Bible Fun Stuff

FOR TWEENS

Classy, Flashy
Bible Dramas

David C Cook®
transforming lives together

Classy, Flashy Bible Dramas
Published by David C. Cook
4050 Lee Vance View
Colorado Springs, CO 80918 U.S.A.

David C. Cook Distribution Canada
55 Woodslee Avenue, Paris, Ontario, Canada N3L 3E5

David C. Cook U.K., Kingsway Communications
Eastbourne, East Sussex BN23 6NT, England

David C. Cook and the graphic circle C logo
are registered trademarks of Cook Communications Ministries.

Written by Kristi Hemingway-Weatherall
Cover Design by BMB Design
Cover Photography © Brad Armstrong Photography
Interior Design by Rebekah Lyon
Illustrations by Kris and Sharon Cartwright

ISBN 978-1-4347-6858-2

First Printing 2008
Printed in the United States

1 2 3 4 5 6 7 8 9 10

FOR TWEENS

Classy, Flashy Bible Dramas

Table of Contents

Introduction

The Gospel message—all of Scripture actually—is story: God's story, our stories, and how they come together. Scripture is full of drama, suspense, humor, human frailty, tragedy, and triumph.

Dramatic exploration reinforces spiritual truths in an active and creative way. Students are forced out of their comfort zones as they work in pairs and small groups to collaborate, improvise, and take turns performing, observing, and sharing questions and feedback. These dramatic activities are designed to help students think and explore the Bible in new ways, and to ask hard questions and personalize their faith.

Classy, Flashy Bible Dramas is chock-full of active, imaginative explorations of Bible truths. Most require only a few props and a simple set. Get ready to teach your students by starting with the Bible background, putting yourself inside the story and asking what God wants to teach you personally. Then turn the page for some easy tips to enrich learning and a list of props and costumes.

You'll find two kinds of dramas in this book: scripts to read and improvisational activities where kids have to think on their feet. The scripts make great readers' theater events, or you can rehearse, memorize lines, and stage full productions for other classes or adult groups in your congregation. The improvisational activities challenge kids to think creatively and get them connected to each other in new ways.

These activities and scripts can be adapted to use in any order as space and time allows. These drama activities can be an alternative Step 3 activity for David C. Cook's *Bible-in-Life* or *Echoes* curriculum—or any curriculum for that matter. Use the correlation chart on page 112 to match a drama to a lesson or use the Scripture Index or Topic Index to match up an activity to a specific Bible story.

At the end of each script or activity, you'll find "Curtain Call." These discussion questions take just a few minutes and will help your students solidify and apply the Bible truth to their own lives.

Taking the Stage

As the director, stage manager, and master of ceremonies, keep in mind a few things:

■ Drama calls for laying aside inhibitions, taking risks, and being comfortable performing in front of a group. Naturally, some students will be more comfortable with this than others. Be sure to establish a safe and encouraging atmosphere. Let students know you will not tolerate teasing or negative comments.

■ Emphasize the importance of being a good audience for one another. Students may be tempted to plan their own presentation or whisper last minute ideas to their group members while in the audience. Require that undivided attention be given to performers, with no distractions from the audience.

■ Many of the activities are just that—active. Some of the games are by nature loud and rowdy. You will find it helpful to establish signals with your students—a signal for silence, a signal for everyone to freeze, and a signal to gather back together. This will save your voice and spare you potential frustration.

Props and Costumes

A prop box and a costume box are both optional. You can certainly complete the activities without them, but they will make things a lot more fun and interesting. They can each contain any random assortment of fun items you manage to collect. Here are a few suggestions:

PROPS
- telephones
- purses
- books
- broom
- handkerchiefs
- prop microphones
- backpack or canvas bag
- nail file
- feather duster
- throw pillows
- kitchen utensils
- clipboard
- a cooking pot/pan
- hand fan
- briefcase

COSTUMES
- costume jewelry/eyeglasses
- hats—as many different kinds as you can find
- animal ears
- scarves—various sizes and colors
- vests, jackets, and robes
- blank white masks

Situation, Problem, Solution

Scripture Verse:
Exodus 18

Memory Verse:
My son, keep your father's commands and do not forsake your mother's teaching. Proverbs 6:20

Bible Background

Moses was in charge of a whole lot of people. It was a very big job, especially since the people came running to him with every little problem and disagreement. When Moses' father-in-law, Jethro, came for a visit, he found Moses stressed and worn out. Jethro was a priest and ruler among his own people in Midian, and he was a wise man.

Respect for elders is a spiritual principle taught throughout both the Old and New Testaments, and Moses had great respect for Jethro. Because of that respect and his humility, Moses was not insulted or defensive when Jethro suggested he change his system of ruling the people. Jethro recognized that Moses just couldn't handle all the problems and suggested that he appoint other rulers under him to solve the simple matters that were already covered by tradition and law. Then Moses would be free to handle only those issues that were more complicated.

Moses knew that Jethro wanted to help and that his advice was good. Have you received good advice from someone before? Can you think back to a time when you thought your parents didn't know anything? Did you find out later that their advice was right? At the tweens age, peers hold great influence, and it is easy for kids to dismiss parental advice. Encourage them to seek wisdom from their parents when facing difficulties. They just may find that parents can help a lot more than they may think.

Teacher Tips

This activity is done in groups of three. A fun way to mix up the class and keep students from just sticking with their closest friends is to call out instructions such as: find two other people with your same birthday month; find two people whose names start with letters either the same as yours or within two letters away in the alphabet; find two people with the same number of siblings as you.

Or you can give students three categories and ask them to place themselves in one of the groups: all who like fishing here, hate fishing there, and don't have an opinion on fishing over there. Then pick one person from each of these groups to form the small groups of three. You'll undoubtedly have uneven numbers and leftovers. That's okay, just shift them around.

Props

★ Prop box, if available; if you don't have one, students can mime objects.

Set

You will need a performance area and an area for the rest of the class to be seated as an audience. The performance area should be mostly clear, but you can make a small table, some chairs, and a box of random props available at the side for performers to use if they choose.

Activity Instructions

This is an improvisational exercise. If your class has never done any improvisational activities, start by explaining that improvisation means creating scenes of comedy or drama by making them up as you go along. The goal is to create scenes with a beginning, middle, and end. The fun part is that anything can happen and you don't know what your partners will do or say. As an improvisational performer, you have to react, go along with what's happening, and try to initiate ideas and action. Young children do this all the time when they are playing make-believe games. Encourage students to try and recapture the fun of using their imaginations in this way.

Often the best way to solve a problem is to ask for help or advice. However, sometimes we don't even realize we have a problem. Moses didn't really realize he had a problem. He hadn't even thought of trying to do things differently until Jethro pointed out that things didn't seem to be working that well. Today you will be working together to identify and then solve the problem. But first—

Use one of the methods described in Teacher Tips to place students into groups of three. If you have an odd number, you can have one or two groups of four. Once students are divided into threes, have them sit down with their groups in the audience area. Ask students to designate one person within their groups to represent the situation, one person to represent the problem, and one person to represent the solution. (In a group of four, one of these tasks can have two people.) They will want to know more details, but tell them to just complete this task without further questions.

Once the groups have made this decision, explain that you will have them come up one group at a time to improvise a scene. You will give the group a setting for their scene but no more. They will be told where the scene takes place, and the rest will be up to them. They will have no time to plan, discuss, or rehearse. You can explain further with the following example.

The "situation person" will enter the scene first. It will be that student's job to define the situation. The students must be careful not to define the problem or try to solve it. For instance, the situation person might be told that he is in his front yard where there is a large rock. The student enters the scene and says something like, "Oh what a beautiful morning to be outside in my yard. I think I'll go get my cup of coffee and my newspaper and just sit on that big rock over there in the sun."

The student has clearly established the situation with this simple line and action. Having heard the situation from offstage, the "problem person" must quickly decide on the problem in this situation and enter the scene. She might say something like, "What are you doing just sitting out here in your bathrobe? We have a lot to do today." The situation student goes along with where this new character is taking the scene.

"What do we have to do?"

"Well, for one thing, I want this big rock moved to the backyard. It's right in the way of where the kids play, and I'm afraid someone's going to get hurt."

"This rock must weigh 500 pounds."

"Then we need to figure out what to do, because it can't stay here."

We get the idea that this is a couple. They have clearly established the problem, so now the "solution person" will enter the scene and solve the problem. The solution person will somehow communicate who he or she is as well. He might say, "Hi, George and Greta. Beautiful morning, huh? I'm just out walking little Buffy here. She never lets me sleep in on Saturdays. What are you two doing out so early?"

They'll explain the problem and perhaps the neighbor has access to a forklift, or knows a way to get the rock on a wagon, or proposes that they get the whole neighborhood to help roll the rock. He might offer several different plans before they find one that works. The group will then proceed to carry out the solution and end the scene. Some scenes will be quite short and others may be longer. Ask who would like to volunteer to go first. Students will gain confidence and enthusiasm as they see their peers performing.

Some suggested settings to choose from:
- A mall with a fountain in the middle
- A car with a drink in the drink holder
- At the circus on the high wire
- At a slumber party in a tent
- A fancy restaurant with flowers on the table
- A garage with a number of power tools
- In a forest next to a river
- At the zoo in the reptile house

Curtain Call

End the session with a discussion on the following questions to help the students reflect back on the Bible lesson, and then go over the memory verse as a reference.

- **Sometimes it's hard to listen to advice, especially from our elders. Why is this?** *(They don't seem to know anything; I want to do things myself.)*
- **When someone suggests that you change the way you're doing something, what is your first response?** *(stubbornness, hurt, anger, resentment)*
- **To whom do you normally go for help with a problem?** *(parents, sibling, teacher, friend, etc.)*
- **What are some things that made Moses an unlikely leader for God's people?** *(his doubt, slowness of speech, his fear)*
- **What are some of the things that made Moses a successful leader?** *(his respect, humility, willingness to listen to advice)*
- **We can find some wise advice in those around us. How can you be more open to listening to advice?** *(Ask God for willing ears to hear; admit we don't know all things)*

My son,
keep your father's commands
and do not forsake your
mother's teaching.
Proverbs 6:20

Inside Out

Scripture Verse:
1 Samuel 14:47—16:13

Memory Verse:
So be careful to do what the LORD your God has commanded you;
do not turn aside to the right or to the left.
Deuteronomy 5:32.

Bible Background

Saul was tall, handsome, and strong. He seemed like a good choice as a king for Israel. Saul led his army to many victories over their enemies all around. But then Saul started to show that he was weaker on the inside than the outside. He made sacrifices that only the priests were allowed to make and thought it was no big deal that he had violated God's law.

Then he disobeyed God's instructions to destroy the Amalekites and everything they owned. He and his army saved the good stuff for themselves. What had begun as a holy war degenerated into a quest for personal gain. When the prophet Samuel confronted him, Saul made excuses and blamed the people. He even tried to put a spin on his sin by claiming that they had brought back the best of the plunder so they could sacrifice it to God.

A good leader takes responsibility for mistakes, but Saul was more concerned about the people's opinion than about God's. The result was that God rejected Saul as king. Saul went through the motions of repenting, but it was too late. Samuel never visited King Saul again.

Samuel left Saul and went to Bethlehem, where he anointed David as the future king of Israel. When Samuel was looking for the new king of Israel, he was almost fooled by David's tall, handsome brothers. God reminded Samuel that what matters most is what's on the inside, in the heart.

Too many times, we have a tendency to look at the outward appearance not only of others, but our own heart as well. We may look good on the outside, but what do we have lurking within? God is always looking for someone who will obey Him rather than one who looks good on the outside. Help your students learn to take their relationships beyond skin deep, looking to the heart of each person.

Teacher Tips

The Bible says that we humans look mainly on the outside to decide what we think of people, while God sees the inside. Discuss some of the things we look for in judging other people.

Clothing is a big issue for tweens. Discuss what kinds of clothing are "in" and what kinds are not. Talk about some fashions of the past, and gently make the point that outward fashions change, so we need to be focused on what really matters.

Props

★ 2 rolls of toilet paper for each group of 2-4 students

★ CD player with a CD of instrumental jazz background music

★ Optional: You'll want your camera for this activity!

Set

Each group needs its own space to work. Then you will want to create some kind of aisle or runway where students can sit around to observe.

Activity Instructions

Today you get to be fashion/costume designers. You get to decide what fashions will make people super cool this year. You will have 10 minutes to create the "in" look for this year and clothe your model with your designer outfit. Your goal is to make your model look really good on the outside.

Start by asking students, both male and female, who would like to be a fashion model. Once models are chosen, then select the designers who will clothe each model. That way you avoid ending up with a group where no one is willing to be the model. You can work with groups of anywhere from two to five students, depending on the size of your class. Aim to have at least three or four different models if possible.

Once the groups are determined and have separated into their different work areas, give each group two rolls of toilet paper to work with. Don't tell them ahead of time or let them see that they will be working with toilet paper. It's fun to let that be a surprise!

Tell the groups that they only have 10 minutes to work. Therefore they won't have time to discuss and debate. Encourage them to just dive in and start designing. Tell them to try different things. Suggest they wrap toilet paper around their model in different ways to create hats, shirts, pants, skirts, dresses, and even jewelry! Designers can roll the toilet paper and rip it into different shapes and sizes to create their costumes.

Each group should also pick one person to ad-lib a fancy, adjective-filled description of their outfit. Encourage descriptions of colors and textures, as well as the mood and overall impression created by this outfit. The more exaggerated and outrageous these descriptions are, the funnier, since in reality all the models are wearing toilet paper!

You might want to read this sample to inspire the writers: **"As you can see, Suzy is wearing the latest from Bangladesh. Her toga-style tunic is hand stitched by monks using spider silk. The fabric is so delicate it must just feel like wearing air. The layer under the tunic is actually woven from seaweed that is rolled over repeatedly by walruses. Suzy's belt is made from yak intestine and inlaid with rubies from the dwarf mines of Tasmania . . . "** And more such nonsense!

When all of the groups have finished, set up the room with a runway-like aisle down the middle in preparation for a fashion show. Each group should choose one of the designers to be the announcer, narrating as their model walks the runway. It's fun to use some soothing, jazz music for the fashion show and to take pictures to view later.

When the laughter dies down, you can finish the fashion show with the following Scripture as a lead-in to a discussion time.

"The LORD does not look at the things man looks at. Man looks at the outward appearance, but the LORD looks at the heart." 1 Samuel 16:7b

Curtain Call

Although this exercise is fun, silly, and creates a lot of laughter, students can understand the point of how meaningless it is to judge by outward appearances. Those judgments are so often false.

When Samuel was looking for the new king of Israel, he was almost fooled by David's tall, handsome brothers. God reminded Samuel that what matters most is what's on the inside, in the heart.

Use the following questions to lead students in a discussion highlighting these truths and go over the verse.

- **Does it make sense to decide what we think of someone based on clothing? Why or why not?** *(No. Outward appearances can be deceiving, good clothes do not guarantee good character.)*
- **What about how they wear their hair or how tall, how strong, or even how smart they are?** *(Physical characteristics do not indicate character. "Smarts" and wisdom are two different things.)*
- **In what way do you hope people will think of you?** *(Answers will vary.)*
- **Think of the people in your life from whom you want approval. What kinds of things do you do to get it?** *(Answers will vary.)*
- **Why was David such a surprising choice as king?** *(He was the youngest of his brothers and wasn't as tall or handsome.)*
- **What did Samuel learn that God is more interested in than the outward appearance?** *(what is in the heart)*

Samuel learned that God sees beyond the exterior that we see. Remember that God looks for the ones who will obey Him. He is concerned with what is in your heart.

So be careful to do what the Lord your God has commanded you; do not turn aside to the right or to the left.
Deuteronomy 5:32

Turns, Peaks, and Valleys

Scripture Verse:
1 Samuel 18:5—19:18

Memory Verse:
The LORD will fulfill his purpose for me. Psalm 138:8a

Bible Background

After David defeated Goliath and sent all the Philistines packing, Saul made David his right hand man. Everyone was happy until David started to surpass Saul in popularity. David was a more successful warrior, and the people loved him. Instead of asking himself why he was no longer everyone's favorite and changing his ways, Saul just gritted his teeth with jealousy and brain-stormed creative schemes to get rid of David.

One of Saul's schemes was to offer his daughter Michal to David as a wife. Saul's daughter wasn't all that bad, but the plan was lethal because Saul asked for 100 dead Philistines as a bride price. He was sure David would die trying. Instead, David killed 200 Philistines. His smile didn't last long, though, because Michal brought even more trouble into David's life.

Saul's next scheme was more direct: he made a habit of throwing spears while David sat innocently playing a harp. God protected David by giving Saul really bad aim. David lived for years with the tension of being God's choice for Israel's next king, yet constantly threatened by the current king.

Ultimately, David was able to wait for what God had promised because he knew that God would fulfill the purposes He had planned for David's life. Just like David, we too have to wait at times to see the fulfillment of what God has planned for our lives. How do you like waiting? Most people struggle when asked to wait for anything, so if you don't like it, join the crowd. Can you think of something that you had to wait to get, but receiving it was so much better because you had to wait? Has there been something in your own life that was worth waiting for?

Teacher Tips

This exercise works best if you minimize instructions ahead of time and just lead it one step at a time, inserting observations and questions as you go.

Start by asking for a show of hands to the following questions.
- **Which of you considers yourself to be a trusting person?**
- **Who here can be counted on to follow instructions the first time, without question?**

Now ask for verbal responses.
- **What does it take for you to trust someone?** *(Answers will vary.)*
- **Who in your life do you generally listen to or take advice or instruction from?** *(parents, grandparents, teachers, friends, etc.)*
- **When was the last time you really had to put your trust in someone else?** *(Answers will vary.)*

Props

★ 2 or 3 bandanas or scarves to be used as blindfolds

★ Large open space

★ 3 or more chairs

★ Whistle, bell, or shaker to give sound signals

Set

Clear all chairs and personal items out of the center of the room, creating a large open space in the middle. Have all students stand or sit around the perimeter of this space.

Activity Instructions

Ask again who in the room feels they are trusting and choose three volunteers from those who responded. Have them stand at one end of the room facing the center. If possible, they should be spaced far enough from each other that they can't touch. Ask each volunteer to name someone else in the room that he or she feels is trustworthy. Have these three partners stand at the opposite end of the room facing the volunteers who chose them. Place a chair in front of each of the partners. Face the chairs toward the partners and away from the center of the room.

Now go stand next to the original volunteers and say: **All you have to do is trust your partners to lead you from this side of the room to the other side of the room where they are, and help you to sit down in the chairs in front of them. Can you do that?** Wait for responses.

Great. There are a few rules, of course. Otherwise it would be too easy and also kind of boring. First, your partner can't move. He or she can only lead you from where he or she stands, and can only lead you with his or her voice. Your partner can never touch you.

Second, your partner can only lead you one step at a time. For example, partners, you can't say, "Walk forward until I say stop" or "Keep going left." You can only say, "One step forward," "One step right," "Get on your knees," "Duck your head," "Turn one quarter to the left," and things like that. Directions must be for only one step or movement at a time. Volunteers, don't do anything except what your partner tells you to do. If you don't hear or understand, then just stand still. Got it?

Third, partners, these people have put their trust in you, so your number one job is to protect them. You need to keep them safe. This is a dangerous journey you are taking them on and you can't let them fall, or crash, or wander off, right? You need to get them safely into this chair. No mean tricks. You wouldn't dream of it, would you?

Fourth, if at any time you hear the sound signal, everyone in the room must freeze. This is just a safety precaution. Demonstrate the sound.

Oh, and one more thing I almost forgot—the volunteers will be blindfolded.

At this time you can make a big production of whipping out the surprise blindfolds adding a dramatic element. As you're blindfolding each volunteer, it's fun to tease a little. Ask one if you can have his skateboard when he's gone. Ask another if he's really sure about this and then fret out loud over what you're going to say to his mother. Ask a girl where she keeps her MP3 and her new trendy boots—you know, just in case.

Once all the volunteers are blindfolded, have each partner say hello to his or her volunteer and practice giving instructions for one step back, forward, right, and left. This will help volunteers get familiar with the voices they are supposed to listen to. Tell the volunteers:

This is the voice you must listen to and follow. Don't trust any other voice. Don't follow anyone else's instructions or you may end up . . . well, I can't even begin to think about it.

As volunteers are having their practice runs with their partners, silently build a maze using all the other kids in the class, chairs, tables, and whatever various objects are available. Indicate through gestures to the class members that they are to move silently and place themselves into various poses and formations to become part of the maze. They will get creative as soon as they catch on to what's happening. Make sure that no one creates a dangerous obstacle or impenetrable barrier. Indicate that they are not allowed to move from their positions or touch the volunteers.

When the maze is set, tell the partners that in addition to keeping their partners safe, they also want to win by being the first to get a volunteer into a chair. Then say, **Ready, set, go!** Wander around keeping the maze silent until volunteers are about halfway across. Then you can start whispering things like, **Don't go that way. Not right, left. You're going to fall. Your partner is tricking you.**

Indicate to the other maze members to join you in the misleading whispers, but make sure they keep their remarks to a whisper. Even after the first volunteer succeeds in reaching the chair, continue the activity until the others reach their chairs. If you have time, repeat the activity with a new set of volunteers and partners.

Curtain Call

Lead a discussion around the following questions to help students reflect back on the Bible lesson and tie in the truths learned in the activity.

- **Volunteers, were you ever afraid? Confused? Did you want to quit?** *(Answers will vary.)*
- **How did you keep focused on listening to the right voice?** *(Answers will vary.)*
- **In what ways was David's life like our maze when Saul was trying to kill him?** *(He wandered in many different directions while trying to avoid Saul and find refuge from him.)*
- **How do you think David kept from wanting to give up?** *(He trusted in God to provide for him and to keep him safe.)*
- **Is it ever hard to decide who to listen to or who to trust? Why do you think that?** *(Answers will vary.)*
- **How do you choose who to trust?** *(Determine whether their words/actions line up with the Bible.)*

Remember that ultimately the voice we want to be following is God's, and we can trust that He will bring His purposes for our lives to pass.

The LORD will fulfill his purpose for me.
Psalm 138:8a

Making Offers

Scripture Verse:

1 Samuel 23—24

Memory Verse:

Do not be overcome by evil, but overcome evil with good.
Romans 12:21

Bible Background

Jealous of David's growing popularity, King Saul chased David and a bunch of his loyal supporters out of town. Saul knew that David was really God's choice to take over as king. Although this was a result of Saul's own failures and bad choices, he still blamed David and chased him down in order to kill him. In fact, Saul was so fired up that he even killed other people just for helping David. Rugged hillside caves provided shelter for David and his band.

Because there were no rest stops in the wilderness near the Dead Sea where Saul was searching for David, he stepped into a cave to answer the call of nature. What do you know? It happened to be the very cave where David was hiding. David could've killed Saul right then and there; in fact, some of his men urged him to do so. But David still respected Saul as king and refused to harm him.

Instead, David cut off a piece of Saul's cloak and presented it to the king as proof that if he had wanted to harm Saul, he could have. Saul was so touched by David's good intentions and mercy that he stopped trying to kill him—for about two days. So even though David did the right thing, the result wasn't good.

Have you tried to repay kindness to someone who has hurt you or treated you poorly? Did you get a better result than David? Even when the results don't match what we expect, we can rest knowing God will ultimately bring us justice if we only wait for Him.

Teacher Tips

You will always have a mix of students who are uninhibited and get creative, and those who are more reserved and likely to hold back. The nice thing about this activity is that no one is observing. The whole group is moving and role-playing at the same time, so no individual performance is required. Encourage students to just dive in. **No one's watching and the more you invest, the more you get back in fun and impact.**

If you don't have an even number of students, then you can participate in the exercise, although this makes it more of a challenge to lead and prevents you from observing interactions. A second option is to let the groups be uneven with the understanding that someone in the larger group will be left out of each round. Just make sure it isn't always the same person.

Props

★ Open space that allows for lots of movement without crowding or danger
★ Whistle, bell, shaker, or something to create a sound signal, or a CD player and some upbeat music for a sound signal

Set

Clear away chairs, leaving the room with as much wide-open space as possible.

Activity Instructions

Divide your class into two equal groups. Identify each group with a name to make it easier to remember. You can use Group 1 and Group 2, but students will enjoy something more colorful, such as colors or mascot names. Get creative, or have kids name their own groups. Have one group sit on the floor and the other group stand.

Explain that the signal—or music—is the standing group's cue to move around the room in whatever way you tell them to move. For example, you might ask them to skip, move in slow motion, tiptoe, walk backwards, sneak, or glide. When they hear the signal again—or the music stops—that is their cue to find a partner from the group seated on the floor.

Approach the "blue" (or other name for the seated group) **seated closest to you. No need to go searching to pair up with your best friend. Partners will be changing constantly anyway. Red group** (or other name for the standing group), **you will first help your partner up and then you will present him or her with an object. You don't need to know what the object is. Just hand your partner something. They get to decide what it is.**

Demonstrate by pantomiming handing an object to someone.

The "blue" team member will take the object, define it, use it, and react. This is all to be done nonverbally. You are not allowed to talk.

As an example you can demonstrate receiving the object, opening it like a small box, taking out a necklace and fastening it around your neck, and then holding it and starting to cry. You received it, defined it, used it, and reacted to it. Give the signal periodically to remind students to move around the room finding new partners to repeat the pantomiming.

Let the standing group continue this process until each person has presented an object to several partners. Then change roles. The group that was standing now sits, and the group that was sitting now stands. Repeat the same procedure of presenting and receiving objects. Encourage students to find new partners they haven't yet paired with, and to receive some new, unusual, and unexpected object each time.

With each group, start to add the following variations into new rounds.
• **This time those of you giving the object are really excited and pleased about what you are handing your partner. You're sure they are going to love it. Go ahead.**

• **This time those of you receiving the object should really overreact to whatever you get. This can be a positive or negative response, but make it big. And remember, it's nonverbal.**

• **This time rather than handing your partner an object, I want you to make a verbal statement. You're allowed to talk. But it needs to be something random. For example, "Today's Tuesday" or "My dog's at the vet" or "I told you to watch out for the banana peel." The more random the better. Then your partner's job is to respond to whatever you say. You can then continue the conversation until you hear the signal.**

• **This time you will start with a suggestion, and responders, no matter what your partner says, I want you to disagree. For example, "Let's eat Mexican food," and you** answer, "Forget it. I heard they use dog food in their burritos," and so on. If you're the person making a suggestion, keep trying to convince the responder to accept it.

- This time start by giving your partner a compliment, and partners, I want you to respond with suspicion. Givers, you will continue to try to convince the receivers that you mean it.

- This time start with an accusation or insult—no genuine ones, they should all be made up, over-the-top, wild and crazy ones, like "Your polka-dot breath is purple" or "You killed the cantaloupes." Partners, no matter what your partner says to you, don't argue or defend yourself. In fact, give a compliment in return.

Curtain Call

A valuable truth of life is that we can never control anyone else's feelings, attitudes, or behaviors; we can only control our own. No one else can make you feel a certain way unless you give them that power. David refused to become bitter and seek revenge. He was able to keep his faith and integrity even while being hunted, misunderstood, and falsely accused. Lead a discussion using the following questions.

- **What were some of the objects you received?** *(Answers will vary.)*
- **What was the suggestion you gave your partner? Why did he or she reject it?** *(Answers will vary.)*
- **What was the compliment you gave? How did it feel to have it rejected?** *(Answers will vary.)*
- **How hard was it not to retaliate with insults in the last round?** *(Answers will vary.)*
- **Some of David's friends wanted him to get even with Saul. Why didn't David hurt Saul when he could have?** *(David still respected Saul as king. David knew God had chosen Saul to be king.)*
- **What helps you not get even when you have the chance?** *(prayer, reciting Scripture we have memorized, seeing others as God sees them, imitating His love and forgiveness)*

Whenever we are faced with situations that might naturally cause us to want to get even, we can choose to leave it in God's hands knowing He will bring about what is right.

Do not be overcome by evil, but overcome evil with good.
Romans 12:21

How Ya Doin'?

Scripture Verse:
1 Samuel 31; 2 Samuel 5—6; 1 Chronicles 13—16

Memory Verse:
Give thanks in all circumstances,
for this is God's will for you in Christ Jesus.
1 Thessalonians 5:18

Bible Background

Although God had chosen David to be king decades before, it wasn't until Saul died in battle that David finally took over the throne. The prophet Samuel had anointed a shepherd boy to one day be king. The boy had grown into a warrior to prepare him for his future reign.

When he was finally crowned king, David likely was relieved that Saul was no longer hunting him, a little nervous about taking over as king, and sad about Saul's death. In all those years of hiding from him, David never considered Saul an enemy, but respected him as his king and father-in-law.

David's troubles were far from over, however. He had to reunite the country, chase the Jebusites out of Jerusalem, and then bring the ark of the covenant to the city as a sign of God's authority over Israel. The ark was the presence of God with His people, and David wanted everyone to recognize that God was in control. Two disastrous and failed attempts to transport the ark left David confused and a little miffed at God.

On the third try, David was much more careful to follow God's instructions, and he was so happy when the ark finally entered Jerusalem that he threw off his outer robes and danced through the streets. You might say David was a man of many strong emotions!

Emotions are a wonderful thing, but sometimes they can "get the best of us." Can you share with your students a time in your past that you experienced an emotional high—or even a "meltdown"? What did you learn from it? Were you aware of God's presence during the experience?

Teacher Tips

This activity is a wonderful way to spark discussion about our different emotions and how we show them. Some of the ways we express emotions are healthy and others are unhealthy. One way we show how we feel is through our facial expressions and body language. David expressed himself by dancing and writing the poetry that became the book of Psalms.

Props

★ 2 or 3 plain white, blank masks, available at most craft stores. (You really only need one for the activity but it's good to have a few extras. In a pinch, you could use a paper plate with eyeholes and a string, but upper elementary kids will be more intrigued with a real mask.)

Set

This activity works best sitting in a circle on the floor. Clear away the chairs and get cozy on the floor, but remind students to sit up and stay involved. Sometimes they tend to sprawl out and disengage.

bossy

lonely

angry

excited

nervous

Activity Instructions

Sitting in a circle, give the mask to one student. Have that student cover his or her face with the mask, create an expression that shows an emotion, and then remove the mask and show the whole group. The members of the group then all try to create the exact same expression, so they're all wearing the same "face." Encourage students to hold the expression like a mask for a few seconds as they glance around at each other. Then the group can all remove the "face" together. Pretend to wipe it off with your hands. Take suggestions from the group of what you would call or name this face.

Did you all understand the emotion that the person with the mask was trying to show?

Have the student with the mask hand it to someone else and repeat the process until all who want to have had a turn. Students should attempt to show emotions or expressions that the group has not yet seen. Once everyone who wants to has had a turn to create an emotion using only their faces, you will all do the opposite.

Now we won't use our faces at all. In fact, whoever's turn it is will wear a mask so that we can't even see your face. Now you will move around the circle using only your body to show your feelings. No one yell out any guesses until the person in the middle is finished and sits back down in his or her place.

Students will tend to stereotype their emotions and movements. For example, a student can hunch her shoulders, drag her feet, and wipe at her eyes to show sadness. Another student might simply jump around to show excitement. These movements do communicate effectively and are good starting points. Ask for a volunteer to go first and choose some easier and more obvious emotions to start out.

You can allow students to choose an emotion themselves, or you can suggest one for them from the art shown on the previous page. Optional: Make a copy of the list and have each student draw one emotion from a hat. To increase the complexity and authenticity of the exercise, ask each student to choose an emotion and then think of a time when he or she actually experienced this emotion in real life. Have the student try to remember the sensory details or what he or she saw, felt, smelled, and heard at the time. Give the student several minutes to concentrate on these details before beginning to move around the circle.

Explain that this is what actors do to help them create genuine feeling while acting a role. If students have a hard time guessing the correct answer, you can either have that same person continue to try other body movements to portray the emotion, or you can assign the same emotion to another masked student and see what that person does differently to show the same thing.

Curtain Call

Finish the session by discussing the following questions to help you review this experience and tie it to the Bible lesson.

- **How did David express his emotions?** *(He danced before the Lord, composed songs and psalms to God, sang and played instruments in worship.)*
- **What are some things you do when you are mad, sad, or glad?** *(Answers will vary.)*
- **What does God think of your emotions? Is there any emotion that's not okay with God?** *(He gave us our emotions. Out-of-control emotions that result in hurting us or someone else are not okay with God.)*
- **God called David a man after His own heart. It certainly wasn't because David never made mistakes or sinned, so why do you think God said that?** *(Because David always repented and sought God's will.)*
- **If God tells us to give thanks in all circumstances, how can we do that?** *(Thank Him even when we don't feel thankful. Realize we don't know all the details of every circumstance.)*

Give thanks in all circumstances, for this is God's will for you in Christ Jesus.
1 Thessalonians 5:18

Three Wishes

Scripture Verse:
1 Kings 3:5-28

Memory Verse:
Trust in the LORD with all your heart and lean
not on your own understanding.
Proverbs 3:5

Bible Background

David waited 30 years between his anointing and coronation. He went on to serve 40 years as king of Israel and Judah. For years before his death, his sons jockeyed for power, hoping to be the one to succeed the mighty David and continue the dynasty. Once again, God chose who would be the next king. He chose Solomon, a son of David and his wife Bathsheba. Shortly before his death, David officially designated Solomon as his successor.

When Solomon took over as king of Israel, Israel needed a temple. They had been worshiping high up on hilltops and mountains. These places were associated with idol worship because the Canaanites went to these "high places" to worship their false gods. When Solomon went to a high place in Gibeon to worship at the tabernacle, he asked God for a "discerning heart" so he could lead God's people well and build a temple.

Solomon could have asked God for anything, but this request showed strong and responsible leadership. God was pleased with Solomon's unselfish request and granted Solomon great wisdom. God even threw in riches and long life as a bonus. Solomon went on to rule Israel in peace, to become famous for his wise decisions, and to build a great temple for worship.

Is there a time in your life when you "took the high road" and made an unselfish request? What about a selfish request or decision that turned out badly? Did you see God's hand or timing in the situation?

Teacher Tips

This script, based on a centuries-old folktale, can be used as a fun, in-class reader's theatre script if you want to limit its use to one session. If you have several sessions to devote to rehearsal, you can have students memorize the lines and perform it as a production complete with costumes and props. If you perform the play, you will want to choose one of the endings from your class session and incorporate it into the performance.

Props

★ Beach towels

★ Beach ball

★ Beach bags, sunscreen

★ Bucket of seashells

★ Small plastic crab or some kind of sea creature

★ Large conch shell

Set

Decorate the room to look like a beach shore.

Cast and Costumes

Four siblings, all dressed in beach clothing:
 Steven—The oldest and he likes to remind the others of it
 Claire—Second oldest and impulsive
 Gemma—Third oldest and a fun-loving girl
 Frankie—The youngest who wants everyone to get along
 Mysterious Crab—An offstage voice

Three Wishes

(*Frankie* comes running onstage holding a large conch shell.)

Frankie: Claire, Steve, Gemma. Come look. I found a really cool shell, and it's big!
(*The other three come running from all sides.*)

Claire: (*taking the shell*) Cool. It's got seaweed on it, though. Let's wipe it off with a towel.

(*Gemma* grabs a towel and starts to wipe the sand off the shell as *Claire* holds it. Ahead of time, hide a small plastic crab or other creature in the towel. Make it appear to come out of the shell.)

Gemma: (*holding the crab*) Oh, look a crab was living in it! He's cute.

Crab: (*as an offstage voice, amplified if possible*) Well, it's nice to know that all that time in there hasn't hurt my looks.

Gemma: (*dropping the crab*) It talks!

Crab: Sheesh. Nothing like a harsh letdown. Was it something I said?

Steven: No way! A talking crab.

Crab: Think you could give me a lift over to the water? (*Frankie* scoops him up and carries him offstage.) Oh yeah, I almost forgot. To thank you for freeing me, you get three wishes. Aloha. (*Frankie* reenters.)

Claire: Did he say we get three wishes? Who gets three wishes?

Steven: All of us, I guess. But there are four of us.

Gemma: Well, I should get one because I was the one who found him living in the shell and let him out.

Frankie: But I found the shell. I should get all of them.

Steven: No one's going to get all of them, Frankie. But I'm the oldest so I definitely get one.

Claire: Steven, you don't get a wish just for being the oldest. You always think you're in charge of everything. I wish you'd just turn blue! (*They all gasp, realizing what she's said as* **Steven** *starts to gasp like he can't breathe.*)

Gemma: Claire, look what you did. He can't breathe. He's turning blue. We have to do something.

Frankie: Make another wish. I wish Steven—

Claire: No! We already wasted one wish. We can't waste another.

Gemma: But Steven's turning blue. He can't breathe. (*Steven is staggering, starting to collapse.*)

Claire: It's his own fault for being so bossy and selfish.

Frankie: (*yelling*) I wish Steven would be okay!

(*Steven gasps in a big breath. They all stare at him.*)

Steven: (*when he finally recovers*) Thanks, Frankie.

Frankie: It's okay, Steven. You're more important than a wish. Besides, Mom would be really mad if you came home blue. *(All smile a bit.)*

Claire: *(begrudgingly)* Sorry, Steven. But if you weren't so bossy—

Steven: It's okay, Claire. We were both wrong. But there's only one wish left now. We need to decide together. It needs to be something that will last. And we all have to agree. Okay?

All Three: Okay.

Curtain Call

The people in the original version of this folktale wasted their wishes, but in the end learned to appreciate one another and be thankful for what they had. Will the siblings do the same or not?

Divide the class into groups of four and have each group write and perform their own ending. If time is short, the class can discuss their endings instead. After the performances, discuss these questions.

- **How did you decide on the end of the story?** *(Answers will vary.)*
- **Did you hear another ending that you liked better than your group's? Explain.** *(Answers will vary.)*
- **Name some things Solomon could have asked for instead of wisdom.** *(riches, fame, strength, power)*
- **What might you be tempted to ask for instead of wisdom?** *(popularity, material things)*
- **Why do you think God tells us that wisdom is more valuable than riches?** *(Riches come and go but wisdom remains, riches draw us away from God but wisdom draws us closer)*
- **What lesson have you learned from this activity that you could use in your own life?** *(Answers will vary.)*

In Proverbs, God instructs us to rely on Him for wisdom like Solomon did. How can you do that in everyday life?

Trust in the Lord with all your heart and lean not on your own understanding. Proverbs 3:5

Talk Your Troubles Away

Scripture Verse:
1 Kings 19

Memory Verse:
I will exalt you, O LORD, for you
lifted me out of the depths.
Psalm 30:1a

Bible Background

Jezebel became queen of Israel when she married Ahab. By marrying Jezebel, Ahab created an alliance between his father, Omri, and Jezebel's father, Ethebal, who was a high priest in the cult of Baal worship. The alliance was a good move politically, but Jezebel was far from an ideal queen for Israel. She influenced the Israelites to worship the false god Baal and even persuaded Ahab to build a temple to Baal. Ahab was not a strong, godly king, but easy prey for his wife's manipulations of authority. The practice of worshiping false gods spread through the nation, and finally God called the prophet Elijah to speak out against it.

Elijah confronted the prophets of Baal on Mount Carmel and proved once and for all that his God was the one true God. The prophets of Baal all died that day, and this really ticked off Jezebel. She was out for revenge and Elijah had to run for his life. He ended up under a scrawny little shrub out in the desert with no food or water. He couldn't understand why, after he had stood strong for God on Mount Carmel, God was allowing him to be chased alone into the desert and killed by Jezebel. After such an exhilarating victory, Elijah was now exhausted, hungry, thirsty, and afraid. He was feeling sorry for himself and ready to die, but God had other plans for him. God supplied Elijah with food and drink, and Elijah continued traveling for another 40 days. He finally ended up in a cave, where God came to him with a clear mission to continue.

Sometimes when we are tired, stressed out, overworked or have over scheduled ourselves, our perspectives become skewed. We can forget God's love and care for us is never determined by circumstances. He is always ready and willing to provide for us, calm our hearts, and refresh our spirits. He never leaves us alone. Thank Him today for His faithfulness and rest in Him!

Teacher Tips

This script can be used as a fun, in-class reader's theater script if you want to limit its use to one session. If you have several sessions to devote to rehearsal, you can have students memorize the lines and perform it as a production, complete with costumes and props.

Props

★ Portable stereo with a microphone for amplifying Elijah's offstage voice

★ Aluminum foil to crumple for static sound

★ Optional: Costumes according to character descriptions

★ Optional: Video camera, if you plan to record the performance

Set

Set up the performance area with five chairs in a semi-circle for the panel. One taller stool off to the side can belong to the host or hostess when he or she is not talking. Offstage, set up a microphone for Elijah to use. A prop assistant can crumple foil when Elijah speaks, as indicated in the script, to create the sound of static.

If you are presenting this as a performance before an audience, you can add a large banner with the name of the show on it above the seats.

Some peppy talk show music works well as background to start and close the play.

Cast and Costumes

Yippee Goldbug—Talk show's host or hostess, very smiley and effervescent, dressed professionally, but flashy

Elijah—An offstage voice, weary and afraid

Isabelle Image—An image consultant, dressed impeccably, lots of lipstick

Rimbo Rockbottom—A real tough guy with a tough guy accent, dressed in military fatigues, bandana around his head, tattoos, weapons

Candy/Carl Carbloader—He or she should be eating something throughout the show

Wally/Wilma Worksalot—A no-nonsense businessperson, dressed in a suit with a briefcase

Mr. Lordofall—A cool character, dressed in normal street clothes

Talk Your Troubles Away

Yippee: Welcome studio audience, and all of you out there viewing at home. We have a mind-blowing show for you today on Jerusalem's favorite TV talk show—all together now.

All: *(yelling out) Talk Your Troubles Away!*

Yippee: We have an amazing panel of guests today—Rimbo Rockbottom, Wally (or Wilma) Worksalot, Candy (or Carl) Carbloader, Isabelle Image, and Mr. Lordofall. Let's go right to our first caller. This is Ellyjaw; did I get that name right?

Elijah: It's *(static)* Elijah. *(static)*

Yippee: Elijah, of course. Excuse me. Elijah, you seem to be breaking up a little. Where are you calling from?

Elijah: From a *(static)* cave at the *(static)* top of Mount *(static)* Horeb *(static)*.

Yippee: Mount Horeb. Wow, you really are off the map. Elijah, maybe if you step outside the cave, we'll get a little better reception.

Elijah: Okay. *(sound of walking)* Can you hear me now?

Yippee: Much better. Now tell us, Elijah, what problem would you like our panel of experts to solve for you today?

Elijah: Well, a few weeks ago, all the prophets of Baal totally got blown away on Mount Carmel because God, the real one, dropped fire from heaven to prove that He's powerful and Baal is just a lame idol.

Yippee: It was all over the news. Go on, Ellyjaw, I mean, Elijah.

Elijah: Queen Jezebel got really mad and swore to kill me, so now I'm hiding. I'm starving and wiped after running through the desert for forty days, but my real problem is that I'm the only one left in all of Israel who serves the true God and now Jezebel's army is going to kill me, too.

Yippee: Okay. Let's go right to our astounding panel and see how they can help you. Isabelle, what advice do you have for Elijah?

Isabelle: Well, Elijah, can I be frank? I think you are just drawing hostility because you must be dressing poorly, and your whole prophet attitude, just says "troublemaker."

Elijah: What do you mean?

Isabelle: To get along with Jezebel, you need to come off as a friendly guy. Have you thought about a new tunic, maybe in a soft blue? And I'm thinking a nice, close shave.

Rimbo: This dame got no idea what she's tawkin' about. Whatchagodda do, see, is yagotta get ya some big ol' M16s. Ya strap 'em on ya back, see. Ya get some grenades, man, and a tank. Den ya just wipe out dat whole ahmy, see. A one-man fightin' machine.

Elijah: Where am I going to get all that stuff? I mean, I'm living in cave. *(**Rimbo** shrugs.)*

Candy: *(or Carl)* I just haven't found a problem in the world that a big, heaping bowl of chocolate ice cream can't solve. With sprinkles over the top. Oh—my—gosh. And some nuts. Boy, it does—not—get any better.

Elijah: I'm not quite clear, Candy. *(or Carl)* How will ice cream keep Jezebel and her army from killing me?

Candy: It probably won't, but what a way to go.

Elijah: Anyone else?

Wally: *(or Wilma)* Elijah, face it. You haven't got a plan here. You need to form some committees to help. You need some flow charts, maybe even a slide show presentation.

Elijah: Uh-huh. Okay. Is there anyone else there?

Lordofall: I am here, Elijah. You think you're all alone in this, but you're not. Some friends of mine have planned a feast and some rest for you, but then I want you to go anoint a new king over Syria, anoint a new king over Israel, and train a new prophet to take your place. These guys serve God and not Baal, and there are 7,000 others just like them. So, see? Things will get better.

Elijah: Wow. You're the first person who made any sense. I feel better. Can I get your business card? I'd like to tell my friends about you.

Yippee: Well folks, that pretty much wraps up our show for today. Let's give a big round of applause for our super panel, and best of luck to our caller, Ellyjaw. Don't forget to tune in tomorrow to Jerusalem's favorite TV talk show, *Talk Your Troubles Away!*

Curtain Call

After the play, review with these questions:
- **What was the best advice Elijah got?** *(the advice from Lordofall)*
- **What advice can you give yourself based on this script?** *(I am not alone. God is always with me and knows the future.)*
- **What's the best reason to turn to God when you're feeling down?** *(No one else can lift our spirits like He can. He loves us and will never reject us. He has promised to be near to the broken-hearted.)*

Look up Psalm 30:1 and see what the psalmist decided to do.

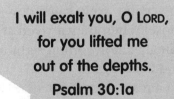

I will exalt you, O LORD, for you lifted me out of the depths. Psalm 30:1a

See What Can Be

Scripture Verse:
2 Kings 6:8-23

Memory Verse:
The LORD's unfailing love surrounds
the man who trusts in him.
Psalm 32:10b

Bible Background

Elisha took Elijah's place as prophet over Israel when God took Elijah to heaven in a fiery chariot. That was quite a dramatic exit for Elijah. It also helped Elisha to know that he served a powerful God and to trust Him. That's why, when Israel was experiencing another attack from her hostile neighbor, the Syrians, Elisha was not afraid. He told his servant in 2 Kings 6:16, "Don't be afraid . . . Those who are with us are more than those who are with them."

Elisha's servant must have thought Elisha was a little nutty because they were alone on a hill looking down at the entire Syrian army. Then Elisha prayed that God would open His servant's eyes to the spiritual realm so he could see the whole host of fiery horses and chariots on the hills around them. As the enemy army came down toward Israel, Elisha prayed again, this time for the enemies' eyes to close! When they arrived at Elisha's doorstep, the enemy soldiers didn't recognize him. They willingly followed him right into a trap. After the battle with God's heavenly army, they never bothered Israel again.

God gave Elisha a marvelous gift when He enabled him to see into the spiritual realm for a few moments. Did you ever wonder why He doesn't do that for us when we really need to know we have spiritual forces on our side? Remember, though, that we have something Elisha didn't have—the Holy Spirit residing in our hearts. God wants us to rely on His Spirit in faith and to remember that "we live by faith, not by sight" (2 Cor. 5:7).

Teacher Tips

This is a wonderful activity to observe brainstorming at work. You are asking the kids to envision all the possibilities for creating different objects. It sometimes takes a while to get their ideas flowing. When they first start inventing objects with the scarf, they will choose ideas that are very "scarf-like." For example, they might use the scarf as a napkin, a blanket, or a shawl. As the activity continues, you can observe their thinking start to break out of the box as they are forced to keep searching for new ideas, and they realize the possibilities are endless.

Although you have a variety of objects to choose from, the goal is to stick with one object for as long as you can, maybe even the entire time. That way the students really have to expand their thinking and way of perceiving. As students proceed through the rounds, they usually have an awakening moment where they realize that "anything except what it is," really means anything. Then the possibilities open up before them.

Props

★ Large square scarf
★ Hat, any style, but durable
★ Stapler
★ Wooden spoon

Set

Separate the group into two teams. The teams should be facing each other with space in the center between them. Each team can gather together in chairs or just group together on the floor. Don't let them see all the available objects ahead of time. Let those be a surprise.

Activity Instructions

Start by asking the students to reflect and comment on the following. **The Bible tells us that we are to walk by faith and not by sight. What does that mean?** Pause for answers. Walking by faith involves trusting that God is in control even when circumstances tell us differently. Often our choices or possibilities seem limited until like Elisha's servant, our eyes are opened through faith and we see that with God all things are possible.

The goal of this activity is to learn to see things differently from the way they first appear. Once the teams are situated facing one another, choose one of the objects (the scarf is good to start with), and lay it on the floor between the teams. The activity will begin with one team sending its first member into the center space to pick up the object. That team member must use the scarf as anything except what it is. For example, Team 1 student picks up the scarf and turns it into hair by placing it over her head and pretending to comb it. As soon as Team 2 yells out the right guess, "hair," Team 1 student drops the scarf on the floor and returns to her team. The first member of Team 2 must now jump up and enter the center space. Team 2 student picks up the scarf and bundles it up, rocking it in her arms and cooing at it as if it were a baby. When Team 1 yells out the right guess, "baby," the Team 2 player drops the scarf and returns to her team.

Team 1 must send the next person on their team into the center space. All the team members must take turns. The team members are allowed to share their ideas with one another, but only if they do it before the person's turn arrives.

Teams can lose members in the following ways:
• If a team member's turn arrives and he or she doesn't enter the center space and create their object within three seconds, the player is cut from the team. Once that player is cut, the next person in line must jump up and start within three seconds, or he too will be cut.
• If a person repeats an object or idea that has already been used, he or she is cut from the team.
• If a team member uses an object as what it actually is—like using the stapler as a stapler—he or she is cut from the team.

• For "cut" team members, you can designate a third area where they can all sit to observe. They are no longer allowed to yell out ideas or guesses with their teams.

You can either call a new round when the students seem to be running out of ideas (although they usually get more and more ideas as the activity progresses), or you can challenge them to come up with as many objects as possible in a set amount of time. At the end of that time, whichever team has the most members left wins. You can then call a new round, changing the object in the center space and allowing all "cut" team members back onto their teams.

Curtain Call

Leave time at the end of the session to discuss the following questions. This will help students to tie the activity back to the Bible lesson.

- **When the activity started, were you afraid you wouldn't be able to think of anything? How did you deal with those feelings?** *(Answers will vary.)*
- **When did you have more ideas—at the beginning of each round, or at the end of each round?** *(Answers will vary.)*
- **When you have a problem you need to solve in life, how does it help to discuss it with other people? With God?** *(others can offer wisdom, we won't feel alone, God's solution is always best, etc.)*
- **Was there ever a time when you or someone close to you thought there was no solution to a situation and then something unexpected happened?** *(Answers will vary.)*
- **Do you get the idea that God enjoys getting His children out of tight spots? Why do you think that is?** *(It helps us learn to depend on and trust Him more. It gives Him the opportunity to display His power and grace.)*

Remember that with God's help we can overcome any fear!

The LORD's unfailing
love surrounds the man
who trusts in him.
Psalm 32:10b

From the Heart

Scripture Verse:
1 Chronicles 17; 2 Chronicles 7:1-10

Memory Verse:
You are worthy, our Lord and God,
to receive glory and honor and power.
Revelation 4:11a

Bible Background

David was a man who loved God and loved to worship Him. David didn't worship out of duty, culture, or habit, but because he truly adored God from his heart. That doesn't mean David didn't sin or make mistakes—far from it. God loved David's true heart toward Him and chose to award David with an important promise: "I will raise up your offspring to succeed you, one of your own sons, and I will establish his kingdom. He is the one who will build a house for me, and I will establish his throne forever" (1 Chronicles 17:11-12).

Although David longed to build God's house in Jerusalem, he had been a man of war, and because of that, God did not want him to build the temple. David's son Solomon fulfilled this part of the promise.

The second part of the promise was fulfilled by Jesus, the King of kings, who descended from David and who will rule forever. When the angel Gabriel told Mary she would bear a son, he said, "He will be great and will be called the Son of the Most High. The Lord God will give him the throne of his father David, and he will reign over the house of Jacob forever; his kingdom will never end" (Luke 1:32-33). David was greatly honored by God's promise to him and responded with a heartfelt outpouring of thanksgiving and praise. What a blessing to have such a heritage!

Are you a man or woman after God's heart? If so, ask Him to give you a godly heritage to leave to your children and your students and, through them, to future generations. Thank Him for the privilege of sharing Him with others!

Teacher Tips

This script can be used as a fun, in-class reader's theater script if you want to limit its use to one session. If you have several sessions to devote to rehearsal, you can have students memorize the lines and perform it as a production, complete with costumes and props.

Props

★ **Scene I:**
Chip bags
Dirty dishes
Comic book
Broom
Feather duster
Laundry in a basket
Throw pillows

★ **Scene II:**
Purses or book bags
Lip gloss and mirror

★ **Scene III:**
Skateboard
Schoolbooks
Pencil and papers

Set

A stage, split up into three scenes.

Cast and Costumes

Scene I
   Mom—Frustrated and weary, wearing an apron and a bandana on her head
   Billy—Clueless, but sincere, wearing regular kid street clothes and no shoes

Scene II
   Benita—Thinks it's all about her, wearing something trendy, carries a purse and pulls out a mirror and lip gloss occasionally
   Trish—Thinks the best of everyone and is excited for others, wears street clothes
   Cleo—Very supportive and enthusiastic, wears street clothes

Scene III
   Josh—An older brother and a nice guy, wears skateboarding attire
   Katie—A younger sister who is not sure where she stands, wears her school uniform

From the Heart

Scene I: *Billy is sprawled on the couch reading a comic book, surrounded by chip bags and dirty dishes while his **Mom** is busy straightening the room, sweeping, folding laundry, and dusting.*

Billy: Mom, that was the best lunch you made me today. You're such a good cook.

Mom: You're welcome, Billy. By the way, when you take this dirty plate back to the kitchen, please take out the trash. I've asked you several times now.

Billy: Yeah, I'll take care of that. *(Doesn't move.)* Hey, that's a nice shirt, Mom. That color looks really good on you.

Mom: Thank you, Billy. Listen, when you're done with the trash, you have some homework to do. *(waits, then says louder)* Billy? *(He looks up.)* The trash.

Billy: *(Looks around as if just noticing where he is.)* Wow, look at this room sparkle. Mom, you're amazing the way you keep this house and take care of us.

Mom: Billy, your compliments would mean a lot more to me if you would do what I ask. *(Freeze.)*

Scene II: *Benita, Trish, and Cleo are standing and chatting.*

Benita: Hannah's party is already tomorrow night. I forgot all about it.

Trish: I found the coolest bag for her trip. It has a special hidden zipper pocket for her passport. I was so excited when I found it because purple is her favorite color.

Cleo: I special-ordered that dual voltage travel kit she needs. I had it express-mailed so it would be here in time for the party.

Benita: Didn't that cost a lot of money?

Cleo: Well, kind of. I had to dip into my savings, but I wanted Hannah to have something special. Come on, Trish. We have to help with decorations. See you later, Benita. *(They exit.)*

Benita: Great. Now I have to come up with some great gift to compare with Cleo and Trish's. I hope Hannah appreciates it. It's hard work being such a good friend. *(Freeze.)*

Scene III: *Katie and Josh are brother and sister. Katie is hunched over the table covered with books and papers. Josh is standing to the side with his skateboard.*

Josh: Katie, come on. Get your skateboard and let's go to the park.

Katie: You don't need me. You'll have more fun with just Tim and Janie. They're much better skateboarders than I am. Besides, I need to finish my homework.

Josh: How much do you have left? I'll wait for you.

Katie: Why?

Josh: Because I want you to come. I like skateboarding with you.

Katie: Really? I always thought I was kind of in the way.

Josh: Why would you think that? We're brother and sister. Of course we hang out together.

Katie: You never told me before you liked hanging out with me. *(Freeze.)*

Curtain Call

We are left with the three frozen pictures on stage representing different attitudes and misunderstandings about worship. An effective ending can be created for the performance by having a narrator read the first Scripture, and then cross to each setting to read the consecutive Scriptures. Have cast members come to life and exit after each reading. Then review the script.

"Yet a time is coming and has now come when the true worshipers will worship the Father in spirit and truth, for they are the kind of worshipers the Father seeks" (John 4:23).

Scene I: "Why do you call me, 'Lord, Lord,' and do not do what I say? I will show you what he is like who comes to me and hears my words and puts them into practice" (Luke 6:46–47).

Scene II: "These people come near to me with their mouth and honor me with their lips, but their hearts are far from me. Their worship of me is made up only of rules taught by men" (Isaiah 29:13).

Scene III: "For out of the overflow of his heart his mouth speaks" (Luke 6:45b).

- **How do we honor God when we honor our families?** *(He is honored when we obey His command to love and honor others.)*
- **What's the connection between saying and doing when we worship God?** *(We worship God when we hear His commands and then actually put them into practice. It is not enough just to say you're going to do something, but you must actually do it.)*
- **How do you see that God blesses those who worship and honor Him?** *(They have peace, confidence, and inner strength.)*

You are worthy, our Lord and God, to receive glory and honor and power. Revelation 4:11a

Gratitude Group Shapes

Scripture Verse:
2 Chronicles 5—7; 1 Kings 8:54-61

Memory Verse:
O Lord, God of Israel, there is no God like you in heaven or on earth—you who keep your covenant of love with your servants who continue wholeheartedly in your way. 2 Chronicles 6:14

Bible Background

When the temple in Jerusalem was finished, Israel celebrated in a major way. The people had waited years for a central place of worship. During Israel's years in the wilderness, the people worshiped in the tabernacle, a tent structure. During the years of conquest and settling the promised land, the tabernacle was located at Shiloh, and other structures were added, such as living space for the priests. This was the tabernacle where Samuel served as a boy.

Now it was time for a grand and beautiful temple to house the ark of the covenant in Jerusalem, the holy city. The ark was God's very presence with His people, so moving it into the temple was a really big deal. Priests made sacrifices all along the route as a way of thanking God. They placed the ark in the temple in a holy place, under the wings of the cherubim, and then God's glory filled the temple. The Bible refers to God's glory as a cloud.

When Solomon went back outside to the temple courtyard, he blessed all the people and pledged that Israel would continue to serve God. He asked God to hear their prayers of repentance when they did wrong. God answered by sending flames from heaven to burn up the sacrifices and offerings, and then His presence filled the temple. The people were so overwhelmed that they fell on their faces to worship and praise God.

The kind of reverence showed by the Israelites in this story is rarely seen today. We tend to see God as our Friend and our Father, both of which He certainly is. But He is also the holy, transcendent, all-powerful God who deserves our awe-filled worship and adoration. Ask God today to broaden your view of Him and thank Him for all that He is.

Teacher Tips

In addition to reinforcing the Bible lesson, this activity is great for helping kids get to know each other and for breaking down barriers and cliques. Students will all be interacting together around a specific task, but the beauty is that no one has to talk. They just dive in with movement.

Observing this activity will also make it apparent to you, as the teacher, who the leaders are among the group of students.

Props

★ None

Set

You will need a big open space. Move all the chairs aside and have students sit on the floor with no one touching.

Activity Instructions

The students as a whole group must use their bodies to make the shapes you call out. All students must be attached to the shape, although they can all use their bodies in different ways. There is no talking or pointing, and no one can move anyone else. Students must simply observe and support what's happening. Shapes go from a simple circle to the more complex, such as a car, to abstract emotions, such as thankfulness.

Your task as a group is to work together with one another to create a shape using only your bodies. You're not each making your own personal shape. You are making one big shape using everyone. These are the rules: Everyone must be a part of the shape. All parts must be attached or touching. You can't move anyone except yourself. You don't all have to use your bodies in the same way. For example, some of you might be standing, another might be sitting, others might be sprawled across the floor, and someone else might be curled into a ball. That's okay, as long as you are all attached and part of the shape. One more thing: you're not allowed to talk at all. How will you manage to work together when you can't communicate verbally?

Lead a short discussion guiding students toward the ideas that one person has to start by showing his idea, and everyone has to observe what is happening around them and look for ways to join or contribute. Ask if there are any questions and then just give them a shape and say go. When everyone in the group is attached and has stopped moving, ask if they are all happy with the shape, and if they are, move on. Start with easy shapes and then get more complicated.

The following progression works well.

> Straight line
>
> Circle
>
> An X
>
> Rectangle (insist on sharp corners)
>
> Zigzag line
>
> Squiggly line (there should only be two ends)
>
> Sphere
>
> House
>
> Car

As students work, praise them for their teamwork. Tell them that because they are so good at this, you are going to give them more abstract words. Instead of a specific shape, they will be making a picture or sculpture to represent an idea. The picture or sculpture doesn't need to be recognizable, but it should somehow communicate the word. They must use the same method of all being attached, with no verbal communication. Just observe, initiate, or support what's happening.

Use the following concepts from the Bible story, and feel free to add your own or take student suggestions.

Worship
Humility
Wisdom
Devotion
Glory
Thankfulness
Sacrifice

Curtain Call

Lead a discussion using the following questions to help students review this activity and tie in Bible truths.

- **Did you ever find it hard to give up your own plan or idea when the group was going a different direction? Explain.** (*Answers will vary.*)
- **Were you always able to find your place in the plan or shape? Was it easy to support and contribute or did you ever feel like there was no place for you?** (*Answers will vary.*)
- **Why was it harder to make the pictures or sculptures than the specific shapes?** (*Answers will vary.*)
- **Solomon led the people in expressing their thanks to God. How does an activity like this help you give thanks to God for what He has done?** (*Answers will vary.*)

O LORD,
God of Israel,
there is no God like you in heaven
or on earth—you who keep your covenant
of love with your servants who
continue wholeheartedly
in your way.
2 Chronicles 6:14

Exiles Against the Odds

Scripture Verse:
2 Chronicles 20:1–30

Memory Verse:
For where two or three come together
in my name, there am I with them.
Matthew 18:20

Bible Background

The book of 2 Chronicles was written about the time when God's people were returning to Israel after being in exile in Babylon. However, they weren't exactly receiving a joyful or peaceful home-coming. They were being attacked on every side by the Moabites, Ammonites, and Meunites. These people were the descendants of those, who in this account of many years before, had gathered to make war on God's people.

After Solomon's reign, Israel was divided into two kingdoms—Israel and Judah. Jehoshaphat was the fourth king to reign in Judah, and he was a godly king who taught his people to worship and serve the true God once again. When he learned about the approaching armies, he gathered all the people of Judah together to fast and pray for God's help. Jehoshaphat prayed aloud to God in front of the temple that was built by Solomon, and all the people joined in, pouring out their fears and their needs to God.

God answered by speaking through one of His prophets named Jahaziel. He told the people that God would fight the battle and not to be afraid. God gave them victory against their enemies, and they didn't even have to lift a sword. This was God's reward for the faith and dedication of Jehoshaphat and his people.

Have you ever poured out your heart to God in prayer and received His answer right away? Even if God doesn't answer "yes" right away, or even ever, we know He hears our prayers and will answer according to His perfect will and timing. As Jahaziel discovered, we can trust Him with our fears and needs.

Teacher Tips

This script can be used as a fun, in-class reader's theater script if you want to limit its use to one session. If you have several sessions to devote to rehearsal, you can have students memorize the lines and perform it as a production, complete with costumes and props. If you choose to perform the play, add some dynamic, sports-sounding music as a lead-in and a closing.

Props

★ Dynamic music and player
★ Lots of junk food: candy bars, chips, soda cans
★ Prop microphones or headsets
★ Toy swords, shields, and armor
★ Table
★ Chairs

Set

The set should be divided in half. The stage right area can be set with a simple table representing the sportscasters' desk. The stage left side should have a few benches (or row of chairs) representing the sidelines. Seat the Exiles here.

Cast and Costumes

Jack—Sports commentator, dressed in a suit with a microphone or headset. Assign this role to a strong reader.

Jill—Sports commentator, dressed professionally with a microphone or headset. Assign this role to a strong reader.

Coach J—He is a no-nonsense cross between a coach, a drill sergeant, and a youth pastor. Can be dressed in either athletic or military clothing.

The Exiles—All the other kids are Exiles. They can be in athletic or military clothing. Either way some of them should have toy swords, shields, and armor. Designate Exiles into Group 1, Group 2, and Group 3.

Exiles Against the Odds

Jack: *(sports music playing—slowly fades)* Well, Jill, it looks like the end for Coach Jehoshaphat and the Exiles. The other teams have bigger and better players. Have you seen the Moabites' new shields and uniforms?

Jill: The Moabites are certainly stylin' for the slaughter. You're right Jack; we're all expecting tonight's battle to be nothing short of complete disaster. With so many of his players still back in Babylon, Coach J's team is looking pretty small and worn out.

Jack: The three teams lined up against the Exiles are in tiptop shape. The Moabites, Ammonites, and Meunites would be tough teams to beat in the best of times.

Jill: Jack, I can't imagine what Coach J is telling his team down there, but they better be saying their prayers. *(**Jill** and **Jack** chuckle and freeze.)*

Coach J: All right, Exiles, I know what you're all thinking.

Group 1: We're doomed.

Group 2: We're sunk.

Group 3: We're done for.

All: Have you seen those teams out there?

Group 1: They're huge.

Group 2: They're mean.

Group 3: They've got really big swords.

Coach J: Okay, okay. I know all that. But I have an idea, see. We're gonna ask God for help.

Group 1: Why would God help us?

Group 2: We messed up.

Group 3: He made us the Exiles!

Coach J: Okay, okay. I know all that. But we're going to ask Him to forgive us, see? We're going to ask for mercy. Mercy is what you ask for when you've messed up and you don't deserve any help. Now, who's with me? *(A few from each group gather around **Coach J**. Those left in the groups say the following lines.)*

Group 1: That doesn't seem like much of a plan.

Group 2: Are you sure it's that simple?

Group 3: What if it doesn't work?

Coach J's team: Stop whining! Coach J is right. Only God can help us. Come on!

(Coach J's team starts jogging in place and stretching. Individuals in this group say the following lines over and over, each time with more voices added.)

All: We've gotta try! We've gotta trust!

(Little by little the other groups join Coach J's group with the movement and dialogue. When they are all together, volume builds into a cheer and then they all stop.)

Coach J: Okay, Exiles. That's what I like to hear, a little faith. And now just to show God we mean business, I need you all to turn in your pre-game chips, candy bars, and sodas. Come on, hand 'em over. *(They pull mounds of snack foods out of pockets and bags and dump them all in a pile.)* Now, all of you drop and pray. *(They all drop like they're going to do push-ups but instead just stay face down.)*

Jill: Jack, I just can't explain what's happening down there. The Meunites keep wiping out their own guys!

Jack: I've never seen anything like it. The Ammonites all threw their spears in the wrong direction, took out a whole battalion of the Moabites, and now they're chasing each other around the field.

Jill: I don't think any of these teams have even noticed the Exiles. Coach J and his team are just lying face down at the end of the field. Are they hiding? Sleeping? What is Coach J's plan here?

Jack: They're all leaving the field. And now the Exiles are running to pick up those nice new shields the Moabites left behind. I guess the Exiles saying their prayers wasn't a joke after all. *(music fade up)*

Curtain Call

During a rehearsal or after the performance, review the script with these questions and Memory Verse.

- **Tell about a time when you prayed with a group of people. What happened?** *(Answers will vary.)*
- **Who do you feel comfortable praying with?** *(Answers will vary.)*
- **Why do you think praying together is powerful?** *(It draws us closer together as a group, it's encouraging to hear others praying for our concerns.)*

For where two or three come together in my name, there am I with them.
Matthew 18:20

Treasure Hunt

Scripture Verse:
2 Chronicles 34:1—35:19

Memory Verse:
Blessed rather are those who hear the word of God and obey it.
Luke 11:28

Bible Background

Josiah really had his work cut out for him when he became the sixteenth king of Judah, the southern kingdom. Josiah was from a line of kings who had not been successful in following God or ruling His people well. In fact, Josiah's own father, King Amon, was such a bad king that his own officials assassinated him. Not only did Josiah lack any example of a godly ruler, but he was only eight years old when he became king.

Despite all the odds against him, Josiah "began to seek the God of his father David" (2 Chron. 34:3a). He began restoring the temple and worship. He first tossed out everything in Jerusalem that had to do with idol worship. Then he began to repair and renovate the temple after its many years of neglect and misuse. It was during this clean-up project that workers discovered the Book of the Law. With this precious treasure restored to God's people, Josiah pledged to keep the law and to lead the people in following God. He accomplished all this by the time he was eighteen years old!

Teacher Tips

This activity is done in groups of three. If you have time, you can use a fun activity for getting students into random groups. Write down different kinds of animals on blank label stickers. Make sure that each animal type is written on three stickers (for instance, three "dog" stickers, three "cat" stickers, three "frog" stickers). Go around and randomly put the stickers on students' backs, warning them not to read anyone else's sticker aloud or to try and look at their own sticker. You might also be able to find animal stickers you'd like to use.

Once you have placed all the stickers, ask students to mingle around asking only yes or no questions to find out what they are. For example, they can't say, "What am I?" but they can ask, "Am I a mammal?" "Do I fly?" "Could I be a pet?" Once students discover their own species, they must then find their two partners and sit down as a group. As a fun incentive you can even provide a little prize for the first group of three to sit.

If you have one or two extra students after forming groups of three, these student(s) can rotate through playing the teacher's role in a round as the "student priest," or have the student take another student's spot in a team while that student sits out for a round.

Props

★ Tablet and pencil for the teacher or "student priest"
★ Tablet of blank paper for each team of three
★ Several sharpened pencils for each team
★ Some kind of small prizes for the winning team

Set

Arrange the room with the teacher's chair or stool in the center and the teams spread out around it, lined up like spokes of a wagon wheel. Lines should be spaced far enough from each other that they can't easily observe one another.

Activity Instructions

Finding the lost Book of the Law was like finding a long-lost treasure map for King Josiah and the people of Judah. God's Word is like a treasure because when we believe what it says and follow the instructions in it, we are rewarded with the treasure of a relationship with God, as well as peace, joy, and salvation. However, it's not some kind of magic spell or potion. Understanding and following God's Word takes work and study. It can be similar to trying to decipher the clues on a treasure map. Today you will be working together to decipher clues to a treasure here in our classroom.

Have teams of three position themselves in lines around the teacher, or "student priest," like spokes of a wagon wheel. If you have a large group, you might want to have more than one wheel. Ask a student to be the "student priest" in the center. Once everyone is in place, explain the activity to the teams in the following way.

The person at the end of each line, the student furthest from the teacher's chair, is the Artist. At the beginning of each round, all the Artists will be called forward to the teacher or student priest. The teacher will then write a clue word on a piece of paper and show the word to the Artists. The word might be a verb, a noun, a conjunction, or an adjective. It could be anything.

The Artists will read the word, but not aloud. Each Artist will then go back to his or her team and tap the team member in front of him or her on the shoulder to indicate that person should turn around and watch. The person at the front of the team should not turn around to watch the Artist, only the person in the middle.

The Artist will then use the paper and pencil provided to draw a picture that communicates or represents the word from the teacher. The Artist must not write the word itself or any letters. He or she can only draw a picture to try and show what the word said. The Artist cannot speak, mouth words, or gesture at all. He or she can only draw.

The person in front of the Artist is the Mime. The Mime is also not allowed to speak at all. Of course, mimes are silent! Once the Mime thinks that he or she understands what the Artist is drawing, he or she should not guess or ask any questions aloud. Simply tap the front person on the shoulder, indicating that person should turn around and watch. The Mime then proceeds to silently act out whatever he believes the Artist was communicating in his or her drawing.

The person at the front of the line is the Prophet. This is the only person on the team who is allowed to speak, and he or she may only speak to the teacher. Once the Prophet believes that he or she understands the word from the Mime, the Prophet may run to the teacher and whisper the word. If the word is correct, the team wins that round. If the word is not correct, the Prophet returns to the team and at that point the Artist and Mime can work together to try and help the Prophet understand the right word. The Artists can still only draw, and the Mime can still only mime. The Prophet can make as many guesses as it takes to get the clue right.

A team that gets the right answer should sit silently in their row until all the teams have finished. You can score each round by the number of teams you have. For example, if you have five teams, the first team to finish gets five points. The next team with the right answer gets four points, and on down.

Once all the teams have completed a round, they can rotate by having the Prophet move to the end of the line and become the Artist. The Artist moves forward to become the Mime and the Mime moves forward to become the Prophet. At this point, you will rotate in any extra students to one of the teams.

For clues you can either have the words of all the rounds be random objects or words from the Bible story, such as: obey, altar, temple, worship; or you can use words from an actual phrase, like obey God, find joy, or just the main words in a phrase like, The Book of the Law is under the table and over the altar.

Curtain Call

End the session with a discussion on the following questions to help the students reflect back on the Bible lesson.
- **When do you find the Bible confusing or hard to understand?** *(Answers will vary.)*
- **Why is it worth the effort to decipher what God has given us regarding how to follow Him?** *(Only God has all wisdom. When we seek God, He is pleased. His Word contains all we need for the Christian life.)*
- **What is something important to you that you have learned from the Bible?** *(Answers will vary.)*
- **Name some ways that you might need to clean up your heart so you can pay attention to God's Word.** *(ungodly thoughts about others, gossip, envy)*

Blessed rather are those
who hear the word of God
and obey it.
Luke 11:28

Passing the Buck

Scripture Verse:
Ezra 7—10

Memory Verse:
He who conceals his sins does not prosper,
but whoever confesses and renounces them finds mercy.
Proverbs 28:13

Bible Background

Ezra was a Jewish prophet. He returned from Babylonian captivity to Jerusalem to help encourage and rebuild the spiritual life of God's people, the Jews. However, he arrived to discover a real dilemma—a problem that had no easy solution. The problem was that many of the men who returned from exile had married wives from surrounding cultures who were not Jewish. These women did not believe in or worship the God of Israel. This was such a serious offense that Ezra tore his clothing, which is how the Jews expressed anguish and grief.

Why was this such a dilemma? For the men to stay married to these women would mean disobeying God further and losing His favor. God had instructed Israel from the beginning of its history not to marry unbelievers because the Jews would be enticed away from God to worship idols. They would also lose their Jewish cultural identity and be absorbed into the cultures around them. However, to divorce the women meant that their wives and children would be sent away and they'd never see them again. Either solution would cause great sadness and suffering. This dilemma was created by the men's disobedience and it brought harsh consequences. In the end, they took Ezra's instruction, honored God, and sent their families away.

It's easy to get ourselves into "hot water" when we disobey God. Even though God always forgives His children when we come to Him in sorrow for our sin, we still have to live with the consequences. Just as the Jewish men had to endure the consequences of disobeying God, we sometimes have to live with the consequences of our decisions. Ask God to gently prod you when you are about to move into a "gray area" that might lead to disobedience.

Teacher Tips

Once you have taught this activity and used it for a session, you can then use it anytime. You can play it in one big group or divide into teams. Feel free to change the topics acted out to suit other lesson themes, or just allow the students to perform general activities. Once they know the activity, you won't have to spend time in explanation and demonstration, making this a flexible warm-up, time-filler, substitute activity, or a fun way to end a lesson.

Props

★ None

Set

Clear, fold, or stack chairs and tables to create a large open space.

Activity Instructions

Often when we have done something wrong, we try to make excuses or blame some-one else. The Israelite men made excuses for disobeying God. They claimed they had to marry foreign women because there weren't enough Jewish women. They may have been angry or blamed Ezra for making them give up their wives and children. In the end, however, they accepted the consequences for their own actions, realizing they had no one to blame but themselves. When we try to blame others, it's called passing the buck. I have a feeling that some of you might be quite good at it. Am I right? We'll find out with today's activity.

Have students stand in a large circle. Each student should have plenty of room to move and not be squashed by people on either side. Place yourself in the circle as well. This way you can demonstrate the activity easily. Step into the center of the circle to explain.

We will go around the circle and when your turn comes, step into the center of the circle and act out an activity. It can be something that you do every day, like brushing your teeth. It can be a sport, a chore like taking out the garbage, something that you may never do like walking on the moon, or even something impossible like swimming in a volcano. When you act out your activity you are allowed to speak; it doesn't need to be a silent pantomime. So if you are giving your dog a bath feel free to speak to her and tell her how pretty she will be when you're finished. Feel free to yell when she shakes water all over you. I will start by performing an activity.

Start acting out silently that you are catching and dribbling a basketball. Shoot and score.

Once I've had a chance to establish my activity for a few minutes, the next person in the circle will ask me, "Mrs. Jones, what are you doing?" I will answer, not by telling her that I'm playing basketball, but with another activity. I might say, "I'm baking a cake." That person needs to jump into the center of the circle and start baking a cake.

Have a student jump in and bake a cake. Once the student has established what he or she is doing, instruct the next student in the circle to ask the first student what she is doing. The first student will then answer with anything other than baking a cake. Maybe she will say, "I'm making my bed." The second student will come into the center of the circle and start making a bed. Have the students complete a practice round in this manner. Once the action has gone all the way around the circle, give the students the following rules. If a rule is broken, the rule breaker must sit in place and is out of the action.

You can't say anything that's been said before.

You can't take more than three seconds to answer the question, "What are you doing?"

You can't say anything yucky or gross or embarrassing for the next person to do.

Since our theme today is passing the buck, you must say things that make you guilty, like robbing a bank, smacking my brother, or feeding my vegetables to the dog under the table.

Encourage students to perform their assigned tasks and activities in the biggest, baddest, most convincing, most entertaining way possible. If one is a bank robber, he or she should be the best, meanest, smoothest, toughest bank robber ever! Encourage students to increase the speed of the game as they go.

Variation: Separate the students into two teams. Have the teams form lines facing each other. The first person in line one will begin an activity, and the first person on the other team, line two, will ask the question, "What are you doing?" Once the team member from line one has answered the question, he will run to the end of the line and the next person in line will step forward to ask, "What are you doing?" The person from line two should answer and run to the end of her line. If any team member breaks a rule, that person is out. The team with the last person standing or the team with the most members still standing at the end of a designated amount of time—is the winner.

Curtain Call

End the session with a discussion of the following questions to help students reflect back on the Bible truths of the lesson.

- **When is a time that you passed the buck?** *(Answers will vary.)*
- **Did you eventually have to accept the blame? Tell about it if you feel comfortable sharing.** *(Answers will vary.)*
- **Have you ever faced a dilemma? Explain.** *(Answers will vary.)*
- **Was your dilemma the result of disobedience? What did you do?** *(Answers will vary.)*
- **Read what God's Word says in Proverbs 28:13. How can you do that?** *(Don't try to hide my sin, confess it to God, turn away from further sin)*

He who conceals his sins
does not prosper, but whoever
confesses and renounces
them finds mercy.
Proverbs 28:13

As the Ancient World Turns

Scripture Verse:
Esther 2:17—9:5

Memory Verse:
Do not be afraid. Stand firm and you will see
the deliverance the LORD will bring you today.
Exodus 14:13a

Bible Background

The book of Esther tells the story of a very brave young woman. Years earlier, Persia had conquered Israel and carried off many of her citizens into captivity. New generations grew up in Persia, exiled from their homeland. At the time of Esther, Xerxes was king of Persia. The Persians did not worship the God of Israel or respect the traditions of the Jews. When Xerxes decided to search for a new queen, Jewish girls were fair game, regardless of how they felt about it. At the end of what amounted to an elaborate, forced beauty contest, Xerxes chose Esther to be queen.

Haman was one of King Xerxes's officials who had come to hate the Jews because Mordecai, a Jewish leader and Esther's cousin, would not bow down to him. Haman came up with a plot to kill all the Jews and tricked the king into approving the plan. Mordecai urged Esther to approach the king and plead for the lives of her people. However, people could only appear before the king if they had been summoned, and Esther hadn't been summoned. To go to the king without invitation could mean death for Esther, even though she was the queen.

After fasting and prayer, Esther went, and the king listened to her. Haman's treachery was revealed and he was hung on the very gallows he had built for Mordecai. To this day the Jews still celebrate their deliverance and honor Esther's bravery at the feast of Purim every February and March.

It's easy to be brave and trust God when there isn't much at stake. Would you be able to do what Esther did and risk your life to do what you knew God wanted you to do? You may never be faced with such a decision, but if you are, is your faith strong enough? Ask God to strengthen you to be able to face whatever the future brings. He is faithful!

Teacher Tips

This script can be used as a fun, in-class reader's theatre script if you want to limit its use to one session. If you have several sessions to devote to rehearsal, you can have students memorize the lines and perform it as a production, complete with costumes and props. This script relies on a fast-paced dialogue, continuous flow of movement, and an over-dramatic, silly style of acting.

Props

★ Stool for Narrator
★ Optional:
  • Furniture to suggest the outside of a palace setting
  • Clipboard for Hegai

Set

Position a stool on one side of the stage for the Narrator. Players will enter and exit stage left and stage right. You might want to partition space by setting long tables on one end.

Cast and Costumes

Xerxes [Zerk-zees]—Interested in being entertained; dressed in a crown and bathrobe

Two Guards—Dressed in matching uniforms, no speaking lines

Esther [ES-ter]—Starts out in rags and adds something sparkly; add a crown or tiara after she becomes queen

Mordecai [MOR-duh-ki]—Dressed like a secret service agent

Hegai [HEG-ay-i]—Flamboyant; dressed colorfully with a flowing scarf and moussed hair

Haman [HAY-mun]—Wears dressy clothes; haughty attitude

Narrator—Dressed in modern day street clothes

Players—Group of girls, mixed crowd of boys and girls

Activity Instructions

Narrator is stationary on one side of stage.

Xerxes: *(Enters stage left, staggers forward with **two guards** and group of boys.)* My queen Vashti is the most beautiful woman from India to Ethiopia. I'll prove I'm not exaggerating. Bring Vashti in here in that new designer gown. *(**Guards** exit stage right. **Xerxes** exits stage left with group of boys.)*

Narrator: That's when all the trouble started. King Xerxes wanted to show off his wife to his friends, but Vashti wanted nothing to do with it. She refused! Xerxes executed her and started to look for a new queen.

*Enter **Mordecai** and **Esther**, stage right, with group of girls.*
Esther: Cousin Mordecai, I don't want to enter a contest to try to become queen.

Mordecai: You don't have any choice. The king's men have chosen you to be in the contest. I'll be watching out for you. *(**Mordecai** exits stage left.)*

Hegai enters stage left with clipboard.
Hegai: *(clapping his hands)* Ladies, ladies. I'm Hegai, and I'll be helping you get ready to meet the king. I've arranged pedicures, facials, body wraps, and dress fittings for each of you. Let's get going! *(Looks at **Esther**.)* You have potential. I'm going to take you all the way to the throne room! *(They exit stage right.)*

Narrator: Esther went off with the women. Mordecai stayed close to the palace to keep an eye on her. Esther won the contest and became the new queen. Mordecai was never far away. One day, he heard two officers plotting to kill the king. Right away he told Esther. Esther told the king, and Mordecai's good work got written down in the royal records. In the meantime, Haman, the king's highest official, decided everyone should bow down to him.

*Enter **Haman**, stage right. Enter **Mordecai** stage left. Enter mixed crowd of boys and girls from stage left and stage right. Everyone bows before **Haman** except **Mordecai**.*

Haman: *(walks grandly)* Make sure everyone bows down to me. *(Points to **Mordecai**.)* Why is that man not bowing down?

Mordecai: I only bow to God.

Haman: *(stamps his foot)* Bow to me!

Mordecai: No can do. *(**Mordecai** exits stage left.)*

*Enter **Xerxes** stage right.*

Haman: King Xerxes, these people are rude and they don't follow your laws. I want to kill them!

Xerxes: Sure, Haman. Do whatever you think best. *(exits stage left)*

*Exit **Haman** and crowd, stage right.*

*Enter **Mordecai** stage left. Enter **Esther** stage right.*

Mordecai: Esther! Haman wants to kill our people. You must tell the king.

Esther: *(shocked)* I can only talk to the king when he calls me. He might kill me if I just showed up.

Mordecai: You are a Jew as well, Esther. You must save your people.

Esther: But I'm scared! Xerxes is not always in a good mood. *(They exit.)*

Narrator: Esther was scared out of her wits! But she promised to fast and pray. She asked for God's help to be brave and save her people. She invited the king to a dinner and told him that she was one of the people the evil Haman wanted to kill. The king did not like that idea! He punished Haman instead!

*Enter **Mordecai** and **Esther**.*

Mordecai: I never dreamed the king would make me his new highest officer.

Esther: Let's declare a holiday to remember the way God saved His people.

Mordecai: Great idea. We want our people to remember this forever! *(They exit.)*

Curtain Call

During one of your rehearsals, use the following questions to review the script with the kids and reinforce the Bible lesson.

- **What was Esther afraid of?** *(She was afraid that King Xerxes would kill her.)*
- **What helped Esther take a stand for God?** *(Her faith and trust in God that He would help her be brave and save her people.)*
- **What helps you take a stand for God?** *(Faith, knowing and trusting Him, being strengthened by His Word)*
- **What does God's Word promise?** *(God's Word promises that He will deliver us.)*

Do not be afraid. Stand firm and you will see the deliverance the LORD will bring you today.
Exodus 14:13a

Trapped

Scripture Verse:
Daniel 1

Memory Verse:
The grace of God that brings salvation has appeared to all men.
It teaches us to say "No" to ungodliness.
Titus 2:11–12a

Bible Background

Daniel and his friends were in a tight spot. King Nebuchadnezzar of Babylon had defeated the kingdom of Judah and taken the most promising of its citizens into captivity. In Babylon, the captive Jews would learn Babylonian ways—food, language, and ideas.

Daniel and his friends were young men at the time, but they showed potential for leadership, so Nebuchadnezzar wanted to shape them into the kind of leaders he could use. The Jewish leaders were to go through a training regimen that would teach them all the practices and customs of Babylon. Nebuchadnezzar wanted the Jewish leaders to forget their past beliefs in the God of Israel and adopt new beliefs, a new language, and new ways of thinking. He made the job very appealing by offering these leaders a lavish lifestyle that included rich and plentiful food and many other privileges.

Daniel was not lured in by these temptations, however. He recognized that eating the Babylonian food, tempting as it was, was the first step down the road of turning away from God. Daniel found a way to stay true to his Jewish dietary restrictions and continued to pray to his God. God enabled Daniel to interpret dreams, and this made him very important to the king.

Have you ever felt "trapped" by modern culture—by its lifestyle, clothing, and morals? No doubt the food of the Babylonians was delicious and tempting to Daniel. But God honored Daniel when he refused to accept what the corrupt Babylonian culture had to offer. In the same way, God will honor our refusal to indulge in our culture, even if it means stepping out on our own. Ask God for the wisdom to see the ungodliness in the world around us and the strength to resist it. He will not disappoint you!

Teacher Tips

Students will be working in small groups or teams of three to five people. The teams must create a scene that has a beginning, a middle where tension rises, and an ending. The conflict in the scene comes from the fact that the group is, or becomes, trapped somehow and they must work together to find a way out.

When choosing your groups, make sure to separate any cliques and evenly distribute those students who are leaders, shy, or particularly creative. This will give the groups a more consistent quality to their work. As they are working, visit each group to find out if they are progressing with the activity. Offer suggestions if needed.

Props

★ None

Set

Clear, stack, or fold up chairs and tables to create a large working area. Each team will need a separate area to work, away from the other groups. Allow students to use chairs and tables in their scenes if they would like to.

Activity Instructions

We all find ourselves in tight spots from time to time. They usually aren't life-or-death situations, but they might be. Today you will all experience a situation where you are trapped. The situation might be dangerous, even life threatening, or it may just be inconvenient and annoying. Either way, it will be your job to work together with your group to find a way out.

Separate students into groups, and once the groups are settled in their designated work areas, complete the explanation of the activity. Students must create a scene that they will perform for the other groups. Give students the following guidelines in creating their scene.

• I will come to you and tell you where your group is trapped.

• First create a performance area that represents where you are trapped. For example, if your group is trapped in a cave, you might choose to work under a table.

• Your scene should have a clear beginning, middle, and ending.

• The beginning of your scene should be an event or incident that causes you to become trapped.

• The middle should create rising action, where things go from bad to worse, and then even worse, and then the worst. For example, you've become trapped in a cave due to an avalanche. You decide to hike further into the cave to see if there's another entrance when you realize that someone in your group has a broken leg. You think you can make a splint for the leg, but then you discover that you left the backpack with all your stuff in it outside the cave and now it's buried. You figure out a way to carry your injured friend, but then the odds are really against you when you discover a bear hibernating in the cave.

• Your ending will show that just when things are as bad as they can get, you will all find a way out. How does this happen? You decide.

• Each of you should decide who you are, why you are in this place where you end up trapped, where you were going before you got trapped, and how you will respond to being trapped. Your movement and dialogue will occur naturally once you decide these things about your situation.

• Make sure that your movement is appropriate to the situation. So if you're in a cave, you can't suddenly stand up or step through a wall.

• Rehearse your dialogue so that only one person is speaking at a time and you are all speaking loudly. Otherwise, we won't understand you when you perform.

• NUMBER ONE RULE—you can't SAY where you are. For example, if you were trapped in a cave from an avalanche, you can't say the words "cave, or "avalanche" in your scene. We want to be able to guess that from all the other things you say and do.

Assign the groups one of the following scenarios:
- A boat in a storm—can't say "boat" or "storm"
- An elevator stuck between floors—can't say "elevator" or "floor"
- A bus in a traffic jam—can't say "bus" or "traffic jam"
- The lion cage at the zoo—can't say "lion," "cage," or "zoo."

Give the groups time to work. Be sure to visit each group to offer suggestions if needed. When the time is up, choose a group to perform first and have all the other students gather in front of that group's work area. Remind the audience not to call out any guesses or to make any comments at all until the group has completed their scene. Then the audience can make guesses about where the performers were trapped.

Curtain Call

When each group finishes, take a few moments to allow the audience to offer affirming comments. You can encourage such comments with the following questions:

- **What did they do and say that helped you to guess where they were?** *(Answers will vary.)*
- **Whose reaction to the situation did you find interesting or realistic?** *(Answers will vary.)*
- **How did this group create rising tension?** *(Answers will vary.)*
- **Were you surprised by the ending? Explain.** *(Answers will vary.)*
- **Did any of the characters remind you of Daniel and his friends? Explain.** *(Answers will vary.)*
- **How did God provide a way out for Daniel and his friends?** *(He had the guard agree to a test to see how they looked after eating only vegetables and water for ten days. He helped them to look healthier and better nourished than the men who ate the royal food.)*
- **What did you learn about looking for God's way out when you're trapped?** *(He is always there and ready to help. God's way is always best.)*

The grace of God that brings salvation has appeared to all men. It teaches us to say "No" to ungodliness.
Titus 2:11-12a

Where Am I?

Scripture Verse:
Daniel 2:1–49

Memory Verse:
Surely your God is the God of gods and the Lord of kings and a revealer of mysteries, for you were able to reveal this mystery.
Daniel 2:47

Bible Background

Daniel and his friends were adolescents when they were taken captive and trained to serve King Nebuchadnezzar in Babylon. Although they grew to manhood in the midst of a foreign culture, language, and religion, they remained true to the God of Israel and to their Jewish heritage as much as possible. They were able to do this, in part, because they were popular with the king and held in high esteem by his court.

Daniel earned this esteem when he was given the chance to interpret one of the king's dreams. The Babylonians considered dreams significant. They believed that a dream could reveal the future, and if it could be interpreted, it could provide the warnings and advice needed to succeed or to avert disasters.

Nebuchadnezzar was shaken and angry when his own wise men failed to interpret one of his dreams. He even threatened to execute all the wise men—including Daniel, who had to act fast, not only to save his own life but the lives of his friends and all the Babylonian wise men. Daniel and his friends prayed for wisdom, knowing that only God knows the hearts and minds of men. God revealed the dream and the interpretation to Daniel, causing Nebuchadnezzar to give honor to "the God of Daniel."

Daniel displayed great faith by asking God to give him the power to interpret the king's dream. He knew he couldn't do it in his own power or with his own resources. So often when we are faced with difficulties, we try to "handle it" on our own. But when we are eager to admit our own weaknesses and lean on God's amazing power, He does great things through us. As a result, He is glorified and others, like Nebuchadnezzar, give honor to our God.

Teacher Tips

This is an improvisational activity that can lead to hilarious fun as the students catch on to it. After explaining the activity, choose a few of your most creative or confident students to go first as a way of modeling to the rest of the class.

If you want, you can do a less intimidating version of the activity by simply putting students in groups of four and letting them carry out the scenes on their own, without anyone watching. If you choose to go this route, you can still ask at the end if any groups would like to perform their scenes for the class.

Props

★ Box of miscellaneous props and costumes

Set

If working with the class as a whole, you will need a performance area up front with two chairs off to one side and an audience area with chairs for the rest of the class.

Activity Instructions

Start by having students share particular dreams they remember. Ask if they have any recurring dreams and give them a chance to share those with the class. If you have a student who's a bit of a ham, you can even have that student come forward and offer a silly, pretend interpretation of a classmate's dream.

Interpretation usually involves taking information or ideas and representing them in a way that helps people understand them. Artists interpret ideas. Storytellers, pastors, teachers, and politicians are all interpreters. Today you will have an opportunity to become interpreters also. You won't need to interpret a dream like Daniel, but you will interpret an event or conversation through the movement of your body and your facial expressions.

Choose two people to sit in the chairs off to the side of the playing area. These two people are going to carry on a conversation and create a dramatic scene, but they can only use their voices. They are not allowed to leave their chairs. Their conversation may indicate being up and moving around, but they can't actually move. For example, one of them might say, "Here, grab this" or "Let's move this chair over the trap door." They can say those things all day long, but they won't do them. They just sit in their chairs.

Before they start speaking the scene, you will privately tell the two people in the chairs who they are, where they are, and give them some kind of conflict or problem that they need to solve. They get to make up the rest. However, they don't have to do it alone.

Choose two more volunteers to help your speakers in the chairs. These two volunteers are going to act out the scene in the playing area. They, however, are more like puppets because they don't get to know who they are, where they are, or what they are doing. They simply move and react according to what they hear the voices in the chairs saying.

Pair up each person in the chairs with one of the volunteers in the playing area. Tell the people in the playing area: **This person is your voice. He or she is dubbing the lines you would be saying if you could speak. So when you hear this voice you must move your mouth as if it was you speaking the lines. You also must move your body and react according to what that voice says. So, if your voice says, "Whew. I'm so tired." What might you do with your face and body to show that?** (Sit in a chair, wipe your forehead, stretch, and yawn.)

Place your two actors in random spots and positions on the playing area. You can then assign your voice interpreters their characters, set, and situations from the ones listed below. Whisper so that the rest of the class, particularly your actors, can't hear.

Remind the speakers to speak slowly and clearly to give the actors time to match their reactions and movements to the lines they speak. Speakers also need to start the scene with some clues of who and where they are so that the actors can jump in. Speakers must keep their hands folded in their laps at all times, using only their voices.

POSSIBLE SCENES:

■ You are two people driving along happily in your cars when suddenly your cars collide. You examine yourselves to see if you are hurt and then get out of your cars to inspect the damage. You are both convinced that it's the other person's fault. Start at the beginning and finish by somehow ending the conflict.

■ You are two siblings who both love television. One of you loves that idol singing show and the other is a big sports fan. Tonight you both come into the family room and settle down with your snacks to watch your favorite shows. You both grab for the remote, realizing that tonight the finale is on at the same time as an important playoff game. Start at the beginning and finish by somehow ending the conflict.

■ One of you is a stressed-out mother of five. It's not easy to make ends meet, so you budget carefully. You enter the store and select several items. The other person is a checkout clerk dreaming about Saturday night at the movies. You ring up the groceries, take the money and give back the change. The mother of five will insist that you shortchanged her by five dollars and you argue back that she's wrong. Start at the beginning and finish by somehow ending the conflict.

■ You are two students in the same geography class. You had almost identical answers on a test, so the teacher thinks one of you was cheating. You are sitting in the teacher's office, waiting for him to come in and confront you. Both of you insist you are in the right. Start at the beginning and finish by somehow ending the conflict.

When you are satisfied that the conflict is resolved, call "solved" and end the scene. You can then choose new volunteers to take over the chairs and the playing space and present a new conflict scenario.

Curtain Call

After several rounds of presentations, review the activity and explore the Bible truth by talking about these questions.

- To the actors: **What was it like knowing only pieces of what was happening to you?** (*Answers will vary.*)
- To the speakers: **What was it like not knowing what the other speaker might say?** (*Answers will vary.*)
- **How can an activity like this one help you trust God when you don't understand what's happening to you?** (*Answers will vary.*)

Remind students that only God knows everything.

> Surely your God is the God of gods and the Lord of kings and a revealer of mysteries, for you were able to reveal this mystery.
> Daniel 2:47

Take Me to Your Leader

Scripture Verse:
Daniel 5

Memory Verse:
I urge, then, first of all, that requests, prayers, intercession and thanksgiving be made for everyone—for kings and all those in authority.
1 Timothy 2:1–2a

Bible Background

Nebuchadnezzar was a proud and arrogant king. Although he had done many admirable things for his country and people, he vainly took all the credit and praise for what was accomplished and didn't give any to God. God humbled him by allowing him to run crazy through the wilderness for several years. You'd think that any king to follow him would learn a lesson from Nebuchadnezzar's ordeal.

In the thirty years after Nebuchadnezzar's death there were five kings. Their leadership didn't last very long. Belshazzar was the fifth of these kings and was the worst of the lot. Rather than defending the city when the armies of Medes and Persians surrounded it, Belshazzar continued having a wild party in his palace. Not only that, he mocked the God of Israel by drinking from the sacred goblets stolen from the temple in Jerusalem.

God shocked Belshazzar by making a hand appear from nowhere. The hand wrote a message on the wall, and the king was suddenly desperate for someone who could interpret. What did the message mean? Daniel, now considerably older than he was when he came into captivity, told the king what the message meant—and the news was not good for Belshazzar. Because of Belshazzar, the whole Babylonian empire was defeated by the Medes and the Persians, and he was killed. The new ruler, Cyrus, and his representative, Darius, were better rulers.

This lesson is about leadership and the qualities of good and bad leaders. Before we can ask our students to respect and follow us, we must show them that we can be models of godly leadership. What qualities has God given you to equip you to lead your students in a godly manner? Are there any qualities you lack? Pray for your impact on your students, asking God to equip you for the important task of leading young people to the Lord.

Teacher Tips

You can use this activity as a short warm-up or closing game, or you can use it to create an entire session on leadership. If you plan to create a whole session around this activity, start with a discussion of leadership. Have the students name some leaders in their class, school, family, neighborhood, city, state, and nation. Brainstorm a list of qualities that make a good leader. Ask the students to think about what God looks for when He chooses a leader.

Props

★ None

Set

Clear, stack, or fold up chairs and tables as much as possible, giving you a large open space for this activity.

Activity Instructions

Once you have completed a discussion on leadership and leadership qualities, have the students sit in one large circle on the floor. Space the circle out so that students have room to move around a bit in their spots.

Today we are going to act like the Jews back in the days of Belshazzar. We are looking for a leader. We need someone who will deliver us from slavery and lead us out of exile in Babylon. Our time here has been bad. We haven't been allowed to worship the God of Israel or practice our own Jewish customs. We are going to elect a secret leader and we don't want the king of Babylon to know who it is, because if he knew, he would kill our leader. Our job is to follow our leader and do exactly what he or she does without letting the king know whom we are following.

Here's how it works. Someone in the circle is randomly chosen as the leader. (You might want to be the leader for the first round to demonstrate.) That person will then start a series of easy-to-follow, repetitive motions using different parts of his or her body. These motions need to change subtly every few seconds. For example:

- The leader starts by bending at the knees in a rhythmic pattern.

- The leader then subtly adds arm swings to the bending.

- The leader, little by little, lessens the knee bends until she is just swinging her arms.

- The leader makes the arm swings a little bigger each time until she is doing shoulder touches.

- The leader adds a finger snap on the down swing.

- The leader starts to step in place with each swing.

- The leader makes the arm swings smaller and the steps bigger each time until she has eliminated the arm swings and is now sticking out her heels alternately with each step.

- The leader adds a forward nod of the head with each step, starting small and becoming more pronounced.

The other people in the circle must copy the leader's movement exactly, keeping up with the subtle changes. The trick is they have to follow the leader without looking right at her. Ask the group for ideas of how this is possible. *(They can look at someone across from them who is following someone else, who is following someone else. They can use their peripheral vision.)*

The reason they shouldn't stare right at the leader is because we are trying to keep the leader's identity a secret from the king. Who is the king? Choose any volunteer and have that person leave the circle. He or she can leave the room completely or just walk a short distance and hide his or her eyes.

While the king is not looking, you will indicate to the group who the leader will be. Remind them that the leader runs the risk of being killed if he or she is discovered. Once chosen, the leader should start moving. When everyone in the group is moving together you can call the king back. Have everyone yell together, **"Oh, king."**

The king will then enter the middle of the circle. The king gets three guesses to figure out who the leader is. If the king succeeds in discovering the leader with three guesses, the leader is out and must sit down in his or her spot. If the king doesn't guess correctly, the leader escapes and becomes the king for the next round.

The challenge increases as more leaders get out and the circle contains fewer people to choose from. If the circle gets too sparse and you want to keep playing so that more students can take turns being the king or the leader, then just call **"Freedom day,"** and everyone reenters the game.

Curtain Call

After several rounds of the game, review the activity and explore the Bible truth by talking about these questions.

- **What was it like to feel responsible to not only follow, but to protect your leader?** *(Answers will vary.)*
- **Did you feel nervous at being responsible for the leader? Why or why not?** *(Answers will vary.)*
- **Why do you think God tells us to pray for our leaders?** *(God will enable them to rule in a godly manner. We will be more tender-hearted toward them. God has established all authority. They may come to know God through our prayers.)*
- **How can this activity help you to remember to pray for your leaders?** *(Answers will vary.)*
- **What does God say will happen to a nation that defies Him?** *(It will be destroyed.)*

I urge, then, first of all, that requests, prayers, intercession and thanksgiving be made for everyone—for kings and all those in authority.
1 Timothy 2:1–2a

Photo Album

Scripture Verse:

Matthew 28; 1 Corinthians 15

Memory Verse:

Christ has indeed been raised from the dead,
the firstfruits of those who have fallen asleep.
1 Corinthians 15:20

Bible Background

It's only natural that people had different reactions to the news that Jesus was alive again. This certainly was hard to believe for those who saw Him crucified. They witnessed the beating and heard the sound of the hammers driving nails through flesh into wood. They had seen the spear pierce His side. No one could survive crucifixion. Could Jesus actually have risen from the dead? Many of His disciples reacted with a mixture of hope and doubt. Others scoffed at the idea of someone returning from the dead as absurd. Jesus' enemies were outraged that His body was missing and His disciples were claiming He was alive. Some of them were probably afraid, knowing that if Jesus really was God and had risen from the dead, they were in trouble after what they'd done to Him!

But Jesus didn't rise from the dead in order to seek revenge on those who had killed Him. He rose from the dead to break the power of death and of sin and to offer this power to us through faith in Him. The offer of His love and salvation was even for His enemies, and it is still offered to everyone today. When Jesus rose from the dead, it was undeniable proof that He is who He said He was. Our faith rests secure on the fact of the resurrection.

Have you ever meditated on how amazing our salvation is? God became a Man and suffered a most horrific death so that we could gain what we don't deserve and never could earn. He actually became sin itself so that we could become righteousness itself (2 Corinthians 5:21). Isn't that incredible? When we think about that reality, thanksgiving and praise to God just pour forth from our hearts!

Teacher Tips

As a class, read aloud one or more of the accounts of the resurrection recorded in the gospels. Use Matthew 28:1–15, Mark 16:1–8, Luke 24:12–35, and John 20:1–8. Discuss with students the different reactions to the news of the resurrection by the various people who were there.

Ask students to consider how they might have responded to the news had they been there. Students will work in small groups of four or five. When choosing groups, make sure to separate cliques and to evenly distribute those students who are leaders, those who are particularly shy, or those who are especially creative.

Props

★ Costume box containing a variety of scarves, vests, and hats

Set

Stack or fold chairs to get them out of the way. Each group will need an open space in which to work, separated from the other groups.

Activity Instructions

When small groups have been formed, have each group go to their designated work area and sit quietly. As a group, they will be creating a photo album of the first resurrection morning. The photo album will consist of at least four frozen vignettes, illustrating what happened that morning and showing the different responses of the people who were there.

In creating their pictures for the photo album, students will use themselves and a minimal number of set pieces and costumes if they want. Costumes and set pieces are not required but they are allowed. Not every group member has to be in every photo, but every group member must be in some photos.

In creating photos, groups need to be aware of the following things:

■ Is everyone's face showing in the frozen picture? If not, adjust your positions.

■ Does the picture show action?

■ Do facial expressions reflect the feelings and emotions of the situation?

■ Are there different levels and body positions used to make the picture interesting?

Choose one of the groups to demonstrate the activity by using the story of Jesus' birth. Do this quickly by telling the students where to go for each new photo. Make sure their faces are visible to the audience and that they are reflecting the appropriate emotion. Each picture should be held completely frozen for at least four or five seconds, giving the viewers a chance to see the faces and absorb what's happening in the picture.

1. In the first photo, have one student standing with arms out and another student kneeling and looking up surprised, to show Mary being visited by the angel.

2. In the second photo, have the student playing Mary stand to one side with her head down and a group of students standing apart from her in poses of pointing and whispering in judgment.

3. In the third photo, have a student on hands and knees as the donkey with Mary sitting on his back and another male student as Joseph leading the donkey by an imaginary rope.

4. In the fourth photo, Mary is leaning against Joseph as he holds out a hand in pleading for a place to stay. A third student should face them and hold up a hand in refusal, turning his or her face away.

5. In the fifth photo, Mary is seated holding her baby, with Joseph by her side. You can pose some group members around as animals and others bowing before the baby as the shepherds.

This is an easy story to portray and will give students a solid idea of their task. Give the groups a few minutes to work on their photo albums. Groups can spend a few minutes discussing the main events of the resurrection story and the different people involved, but as always, encourage them not to spend too much time discussing. Ideas flow better when you just dive in and start moving.

Remind groups that each picture needs to be held with no movement for five seconds. Groups can decide on a word or signal to indicate when they will all move into position for the next photo. Groups should move smoothly and swiftly from one picture to the next. This requires practicing the whole series of pictures several times. This means groups only have a short time to create all their pictures and then rehearse them several times.

Ask students to end their presentation by creating a final picture that shows their own responses to Jesus' resurrection.

Curtain Call

End the session with a discussion of the following questions to help students personalize the importance of the resurrection.

- **Have you had someone close to you die?** *(Answers will vary.)*
- **What would it be like if that person suddenly appeared to you alive?** *(shocking, scary, exciting, unbelievable)*
- **The Apostle Paul said that without the resurrection our faith in Christ would be meaningless (1 Cor. 15:13–19). What do you think he meant?** *(He meant that without the resurrection, we would still be living in sin and separated from God. Also, if Christ wasn't raised from the dead, then He and the prophets were not telling the truth.)*
- **How does being a Christian affect how you feel about death?** *(Answers will vary.)*

Christ has indeed
been raised from the dead,
the firstfruits of those
who have fallen asleep.
1 Corinthians 15:20

Bethlehem Broadcast

Scripture Verse:
Luke 2:1-20; Acts 13:22-23; Romans 8:3-5; Ephesians 2:6-8

Memory Verse:
Today in the town of David a Savior
has been born to you; he is Christ the Lord.
Luke 2:11

Bible Background

Most people have heard the story of Christ's birth, even if they don't go to church. The most well-known version is found in the New Testament book of Luke. The author of this book was a traveling companion of Paul. He was a doctor with an avid interest in history. While Luke was a stickler for getting the details straight, Paul wanted to make sure that people understood the significance of Christ's birth, as well as His life, teachings, death, and resurrection.

Today it is easy to view the nativity story as just another holiday tradition. Paul knew that it is so much more than a tradition or a nice story. He understood that because Jesus fulfilled the requirements of the law, salvation was open to everyone, not just to the Jews. Paul taught over and over in his New Testament letters that God is not keeping score and that His love and approval are not earned by keeping a bunch of rules. It's a gift. This was really good news to Jews who were bound by all the rules and laws of the Old Covenant. No one could keep them all. Salvation by grace was a mind-blowing gift for them, just as it is for us.

It's easy to forget that salvation is by grace alone. Our human natures want to do something to earn it and to keep it. We want to do "our part" in the process of salvation, maybe because we really want to get at least part of the credit! But God has told us that His grace and the faith that He produces are "the gift of God—not by works, so that no one can boast" (Eph. 2:8-9). Thank God today for His incredible gift!

Teacher Tips

Start by asking kids if any of them ever watch the news. You could discuss certain big events that have been in the news recently and see what details the class can recall. However, steer discussion away from overt violence or anything that could frighten some of the kids. Ask them to brainstorm about what kind of people they see on the news. Guide them toward the answers of anchorman or woman, reporters, weatherman or woman, sports broadcaster, eyewitnesses, and experts.

Props

★ Some kind of small table or desk to be used as a news desk

★ Bibles

★ Optional:
>   Video camera
>   Pencils and paper
>   Prop microphone
>   Costume box with scarves, shawls, hats, wigs, or animal ears
>   Chalkboard or whiteboard to use as a weather map
>   Large paper and markers

Set

Set up the room so that each part of the newscast happens in a different area. This will allow students to present the newscast without pauses or the need to move anything. One area should be the news desk, one area with a white or chalkboard for the weather report, one area for the sports broadcasts, and however many areas you need for on-the-scene reporters conducting eyewitness and expert interviews.

Activity Instructions

Today you will have the opportunity to recreate the evening news in Bethlehem on the night that Jesus was born. In a newscast, the anchorman or woman welcomes you to the station and then goes right into the top story—whatever is big news. Then you have stories where the anchor speaks with reporters on the scene. You might have a weather report and a sports update. You will usually see a happy human-interest story and some news about local issues or government. So let's think about all the different things that happened in Bethlehem at Jesus' birth that could be part of our newscast.

Provide Bibles, and let students review the details of the story from Luke 2. Some ideas are:
Complaints about the lack of accommodations for the many out-of-town visitors
The strange appearance of a bright star
Shepherds saying they hear music from the sky. Are they crazy?
The arrival of royalty from the east
A baby born in a barn
Herod is not happy about a rumored threat to his throne

Take more suggestions from the students. If you have a large group, you could divide into two or three smaller groups and do separate newscasts representing different channels. Once you have a good list of events to choose from, the group or groups should select roles. If you anticipate disagreement over this, then just ask for volunteers for each role and choose from the raised hands.
Anchorman (or woman)
Reporter(s) on the scene
Eyewitness(es)
Expert(s)
Sportscaster
Weatherman (or woman)

Next the group(s) should work together to decide which stories they will include in the newscast and in what order they will report them. They can write down their ideas or dialogue, but they don't need to write out an exact script. Encourage them to use "broadcast voices" and language such as:

"Jessica, tonight Bethlehem officials are concerned over some strange sightings of creatures over the fields outside of town. I have a shepherd here who was actually in the field tending his flocks at the time. He saw the creatures very clearly, given the abnormal brightness tonight. You'll hear about that later from Joe, our weatherman. This shepherd says that the creatures were angels and that one actually spoke to him. Tell us, sir, just what you heard."
Or,
"We're here talking to Dr. Sheepengoat, who is an expert on the psychological effects of staying awake all night sitting in cold fields. Doctor, what do you have to say about these shepherds' claims to have heard music from the sky?"

Let the group(s) work independently for a brief time to compile and rehearse their broadcasts. Encourage them to think of the events as if they were happening for the first time. What would be their opinions or feelings about the people involved and the events themselves? After they have settled on their roles, order, and rough idea of the actual dialogue, invite kids to gather prop and costume items from those you have made available. Each group can also use the paper and markers to create a sign with the name and logo of their TV station. The sign can be hung from the front of the news desk.

Filming the broadcast creates anticipation and motivates the kids to work hard and be creative and original. You can save the recording to view at another time, or you can watch it right away. If you have editing skills, you can even work to add music and graphics to the recording. If you don't have a video camera, simply enjoy the live performance of the broadcast. If you have more than one group, they can be audiences for each other.

Curtain Call

Often the people who bring us the news only have limited information. Most of the people present at Jesus' birth probably had no idea of how big of an event it really was. Many people today still don't understand the significance.

If time permits, close with a discussion of the following questions in order to help students reflect on the biblical lesson and make the birth of Christ more personal to them.

- **Can you believe everything you hear on the news? Why or why not?** *(No. Everything is being reported from someone's point of view and may not be exactly the way it happened.)*
- **What would you have thought of the shepherd's story?** *(amazed, skeptical, excited)*
- **What if some strange bright object appeared tonight over your house? How might you respond?** *(Answers will vary.)*
- **How does Jesus' birth affect you personally?** *(Answers will vary.)*
- **Is the message of the birth of Jesus restricted to only a few? Why or why not?** *(No. Jesus came to this world so that everyone could have a relationship with God. The Bible assures us that salvation is available to everyone.)*

Today in the town of David a Savior has been born to you; he is Christ the Lord.
Luke 2:11

Eternity Travel Agency

Scripture Verse:
John 14:1-3, 18-20; Acts 1:6-11

Memory Verse:
We know that the one who raised the Lord Jesus from the dead will also raise us with Jesus and present us with you in his presence.
2 Corinthians 4:14

Bible Background

Jesus' disciples were confused! Even though Jesus had been teaching about the Messiah and the kingdom of God for three years, His closest followers still didn't understand that His death would be part of God's plan. On the night of the Last Supper, Jesus gathered His disciples for the Passover meal and spoke words of comfort about the events that were soon to happen. He alluded once again to His departure and the promise of everlasting life.

After His resurrection, Jesus appeared to the disciples and more than 500 other people as well. Jesus spent forty days comforting and instructing His followers before He ascended into heaven. His earthly ministry was over, but there was still a lot of work to do to bring the kingdom of God to the lives of individual people.

When He left, Jesus promised His followers the Holy Spirit would come and empower them. He told them to spread the Gospel to every tribe and tongue, and He promised to return to them. Acts 2 tells about the dramatic arrival of the Holy Spirit as believers gathered to worship. The book goes on to tell about the start of the church, as the now courageous and zealous disciples spread the good news of salvation to the world.

Many people never think about heaven or they think it will be a long time before they go there. Others aren't sure they'll get to heaven at all. What do you think of when heaven is mentioned? Is it a joy to you or are you fearful about it? Take some time today to ask God to make heaven real to you and rejoice in it!

Teacher Tips

This script can be used as a fun, in-class reader's theater script if you want to limit its use to one session. If you have several sessions to devote to rehearsal, you can have students memorize the lines and perform it as a production, complete with costumes and props.

Props

★ Bible
★ 3 airline-type tickets
★ Paper that says "Admission of Guilt" at the top
★ Bell/chimes

Set

Construct some kind of counter that Angie can stand behind. This is preferable to having her sit behind a desk, if you are performing for an audience. You'll need just one entrance and exit opposite of the counter. Use the bell or chimes to indicate each time someone enters or exits. If you don't have an actual door, the sound cue will help to indicate one. A student can be the props person and ring the bell.

Cast and Costumes

Angie—An angel dressed as a travel agent
Man—A businessman in a suit with a briefcase
Woman—A free spirit dressed in something trendy
Mr. & Mrs.—Could be any couple from anywhere
Three Friends—Any combination of males or females will work

Eternity Travel Agency

Angie: Welcome to Eternity Travel. How can I help you?

Man: I'd like to book a ticket to heaven.

Angie: That's what we're here for.

Man: Great. I'd like that for August 4, 2027. I'll need to depart about 2:30 p.m.

Angie: I'm sorry sir. You're not allowed to specify your date or time of travel.

Man: What kind of service is that? How can I plan a trip to heaven if I don't know when I'm leaving?

Angie: We advise that you be prepared to depart at any time, on any day.

Man: Be ready to leave for heaven at any time? That's crazy. I'd have to be willing to drop everything at a moment's notice.

Angie: That's right, sir.

Man: Well, in that case, I don't think I'll book the ticket after all. Having to be prepared all the time would keep me busy every day. I'd better hold off until I have the time. *(Exits, passing a **Woman** on her way in.)*

Woman: Hi. I need a roundtrip ticket to heaven.

Angie: I'm sorry, Miss. We only issue one-way tickets.

Woman: One way? Well, I just wanted to go check it out. You know, find out who's there, if it's fun, how's the pizza . . . stuff like that. I'm not really planning on staying.

Angie: You can actually find out a lot about heaven from our travel brochure. *(Hands her a Bible.)*

Woman: Wow, that's an awfully thick brochure. I'm a seeing-is-believing kind of girl. If you can't give me a roundtrip ticket, I think I'll pass. *(Exits, passes **Mr.** and **Mrs.** entering.)*

Mr.: We'd like two tickets, please. We heard they're free.

Angie: That's right, sir. I'll just need you both to sign here.

Mrs.: *(reads)* But this says that we admit to being guilty. I'm not admitting to any guilt just to get a ticket to heaven.

Mr.: There must be other ways to get hold of a ticket without being accused of . . . well . . . sin. *(They storm out, passing a group of **Three Friends** on their way in.)*
Friend 1: We're here for some tickets. And we've got the cash.

Angie: I'm sorry. We don't accept cash.

Friend 2: How can anyone not accept cash? Cash is real money.

Friend 3: Never mind. Here, put it on my credit card.

Angie: I'm sorry; we don't accept credit cards or checks either.

Friend 2: Well then, how are we supposed to pay for our tickets, lady?

Angie: Oh, you don't pay for your tickets.

Friend 3: Did we win a prize for being the 100th customer or something?

Angie: No prize. The tickets are both priceless and free.

Friend 2: How can they be priceless and free at the same time? Is this some kind of scam?

Angie: The tickets are a gift. *(She holds them out.)*

Friend 3: A gift, my eye. This has to be some kind of rip-off. Let's get out of here.

Angie: *(sighs)* The most amazing all-expense paid trip in the history of the world, and I can't give away a single ticket. *(Shakes her head, begins to hum "Amazing Grace.")*

Curtain Call

Review the drama with these discussion questions.

- **How do you think Jesus' disciples felt when He told them He was getting a place ready for them in heaven?** *(excited, curious, sad that He was leaving)*
- **Why do you think it's hard for some people to accept God's free gift of eternal life?** *(they don't believe it, they're too stubborn and selfish to make a change and follow God, they want to earn it)*
- **Name one thing you're looking forward to about heaven.** *(Answers will vary.)*
- **What does God promise for those who believe in Jesus?** *(God promises everlasting life and eternity with Him.)*

We know that the one who raised the Lord Jesus from the dead will also raise us with Jesus and present us with you in his presence.
2 Corinthians 4:14

Transformation Station

Scripture Verse:
Acts 7:58; 8:1-4; 9:1-22; 22:12-16

Memory Verse:
Therefore, if anyone is in Christ, he is a new creation;
the old has gone, the new has come!
2 Corinthians 5:17

Bible Background

Saul's transformation from a murderous Jewish leader and Pharisee to a passionate follower and preacher of Jesus is one of the most well-known stories in the Bible. In fact, often people who undergo a dramatic change of thought and behavior are said to have had a "Damascus road" experience. This refers to when Saul was struck blind on the road to Damascus and confronted by Christ Himself.

We first meet Saul in the Bible when he is watching the stoning of Stephen, a follower of Jesus and one of the men selected to serve as deacons in the Jerusalem community of believers. Stephen was chosen because he was known to be full of the Spirit and wisdom (Acts 6:3-5). He was a bold preacher who also performed signs and wonders, and this ministry got him in trouble with the Jewish leaders. Stephen was killed for telling people that Jesus is the Messiah. Saul, among others, considered this teaching to be blasphemy.

The death of Stephen launched a furious outbreak of the persecution of believers, and Saul was at the heart of the movement. His mission in life was to kill Christians! Then Jesus Himself appeared to Saul while he was traveling between Jerusalem and Damascus. After meeting Jesus on the road, Saul's name was changed to Paul, and he began preaching about Jesus even more zealously than he had preached against Him.

What happens to create such dramatic change in a person? What kind of transformation did you experience when Christ came into your life? Share your experience with your students.

Teacher Tips

It's fun to start by talking about all the gadgets and gizmos that we use in our daily lives. You could even brainstorm together a list of all the machines we use to make our lives easier and to complete tasks faster. What tasks would be easier if we had machines to help us do them? Ask students what machine they would like to invent or see invented. Many will suggest a homework machine or a room-cleaning machine or maybe a mute button for their brother or sister.

Props

★ Chairs and tables
★ Variety of simple items: scarves, sheets or blankets, kitchen utensils, tools, rope or yarn, brooms or mops, garden tools. Gather as many of these items as you can.

Set

Each group will require its own space to work in. You might assign groups to the four corners of the room, for instance. Clear out furniture except for whatever pieces each group is using in their machine. Make other items available at the center of the room, and let each group choose four or five items to include.

...and then the coaxial renumeration switch gets thrown which causes a chain reaction...

Activity Instructions

Divide the class into small groups of three to five students. Mix the class in the small groups; make sure that best friends don't all end up together in one group with the shy kids and loners standing aside looking uncomfortable.

Tell students their job is to build a machine that will transform the human heart. They will work together as a team, using their bodies as parts of the machine as well as any other items they would like to include, like chairs, tables, and any other random items you are able to provide.

Each machine should have moving parts. It should make noise/sounds. Each team needs to build a machine, demonstrate how a person uses or goes through the machine, and explain how the machine actually works to transform a heart. The more technical, medical-sounding, long, spiritual words they use in their explanation, the better.

Give the teams 10 to 15 minutes to build their machines. Encourage them not to spend much time in discussion, but just to jump in and start building. They can start experimenting to see what works. This will get their ideas flowing better than just sitting and talking. It works best if one person in each group does the explanation when demonstrating, but all members should feel free to contribute ideas to what will be said. Remind the students not to build anything that is likely to fall or harm anyone.

Once the teams have spent a short time building, you can have the groups move from corner to corner so each group can demonstrate and explain their transformation station to the rest of the class. They can use a volunteer from the class to try out each machine. Once they have a volunteer, it's fun to set up the transformation by asking a few questions such as:

Okay volunteer, what would you really like to be transformed about your heart? (If the volunteer doesn't answer, just fill in the blank yourself with something funny.) **What's that you say? You hate the color green? That must cause problems since there is so much green in the world. Let's see if this group's machine will work for you.**

Position the volunteer within the machine, if that's possible. Let the whole class provide sound effects while the machine is "working." Once the demonstration is complete, make an observation that shows that the machine has changed the volunteer's heart. **You love green? You want to hug and kiss everyone wearing green? You want to eat the leaves off trees? Wonderful! The machine is successful! Let's go see the next one.**

Continue rotating until all the groups have demonstrated their machines, complete with a volunteer transformation and an amusing narration of the process.

Curtain Call

Lead a discussion using the following questions to review this activity and tie in Bible truths.

- **Machines can't really change hearts. What can?** *(Only God can change people's hearts.)*
- **In Saul's case, meeting Jesus changed his heart. What does God do to change our hearts?** *(gives us a new nature, changes the way we look at things, sends the Holy Spirit to live in our hearts)*
- **How has your heart changed in some way?** *(Answers will vary.)*
- **Have you ever met someone who has had a Damascus road kind of experience? Tell about that person.** *(Answers will vary.)*
- **If you did have a Transformation Station, how would you use it?** *(Answers will vary.)*

Therefore,
if anyone is in Christ,
he is a new creation;
the old has gone,
the new has come!
2 Corinthians 5:17

What's That You Say?

Scripture Verse:
Acts 17

Memory Verse:
So is my word that goes out from my mouth:
It will not return to me empty, but will accomplish
what I desire and achieve the purpose for which I sent it.
Isaiah 55:11

Bible Background

Paul preached in many different towns throughout his missionary journeys. Although his message didn't change, he used different ways to communicate, depending on whom he was speaking or writing to. Different kinds of people had different responses to his message, just as people respond differently to the Gospel today. In Thessalonica a few Jews, but many more Gentiles, became believers in Christ as a result of Paul's message. In Berea, a smaller town south of Thessalonica, the Jews were more open-minded. When they turned to the Scriptures to investigate what Paul said, they found it to be true and they believed.

Athens was a big city where many of the accepted ideas of the times originated. People there liked to discuss and debate spiritual and philosophical issues. This made it easy for Paul to approach them about their beliefs. However, it was more difficult to convince them of the truth of Jesus being the Messiah since they had so many other ideas to choose from. Many of them already had strong beliefs in other gods and it was hard for them to change their minds. However, Paul kept presenting the truth and eventually many of the sophisticated leaders and philosophers in Athens also believed.

Probably even more than in Paul's day, there are many false ideas and philosophies "floating around" today. Are you ever tempted to believe them or at least to incorporate them into your Christian beliefs? Spend some time thinking about how much influence the culture has on your core beliefs. Then ask God to strengthen your faith so that you won't be "blown here and there by every wind of teaching" (Eph. 4:14).

Teacher Tips

The first part of this activity can include everyone and is fun and non-threatening. The second part, however, will depend on having a few kids who are outgoing, have a sense of humor, and don't mind getting up in front of the group and being silly. If you have those willing and adventurous students, you can have a hysterical time.

Start by pairing the students with partners. If you don't have an even number of students, you can participate by being someone's partner. Talk to them about how communication can often be a challenge. Differences in culture, language, and backgrounds can influence the way we understand something or how we view a new idea. Even in our own culture, language, neighborhood, and family, we often have misunderstandings. We just don't get what someone else means, and they don't get us. Paul faced this all the time while trying to share the Gospel with people.

Props

★ A whistle, bell, or triangle to give a sound signal; if you don't have one, you can always just loudly say, "Stop" or "Switch"

Set

Kids will be working with partners to start and then will create a performance area. The best set is made up of chairs and small furniture that kids can move easily.

Activity Instructions

In pairs, have students decide which of them will start and who will go second. Give them a topic they will speak on with their partners, as if they were giving a lecture. Topics can be anything from "All about Frogs," "Safety in a Storm," "Building Things Out of Noodles," or "The Difference Between Jesus and All Those Other Gods." Make up your own, or have students suggest topics.

When you say, "Start" or give the sound signal, the first person will start to talk about the topic. When you give the sound signal again, the second partner should continue talking about the topic, picking up exactly where the first partner stopped, even if it was the middle of a word or sentence. Continue to give the signal, letting partners go back and forth several times. Finally say, "Stop," and whoever's turn it is must conclude the lecture. If you observe a set of partners who do this well and are willing to demonstrate, give them a topic and let them improvise it for the group.

Here's a sample script you might share with students. Ask a volunteer to demonstrate with you.

Person 1: Today we're here to talk about frogs. Now there are many different kinds of *(ding)*

Person 2: recipes to use when cooking a frog. One of my favorites requires a great amount of skill and patience as well as *(ding)*

Person 1: a pound of raisins. Now the raisins need to be imported from Zambia because they have the largest and juiciest raisins, which are really important for *(ding)*

Person 2: Frog a la Raison, which is the recipe we'll be telling you about. Now as far as the frog goes, you want to find one that has *(ding)*

Person 1: purple spots and a confident jump. Confident jumpers really have the sweetest *(ding)*

How will this end? That will be up to the partners to decide for their own lectures. Often the lectures end up having very little to do with the original topic. No problem. It can be more fun to see what strange directions the lectures take.

The next level of the activity calls for each set of partners to trade back and forth after each word. Give them a topic and let them go, no signals needed. After a few minutes you can tell them to conclude and the pairs must work together to bring the lecture to a logical conclusion. Again, you can have a willing set of partners perform a lecture for the whole group, but give them a new topic so that their ideas are fresh.

The third part of the activity is more of a performance. Choose two brave volunteers. They don't have to be partners from the first two levels. Choose students you know will really go for it and not be embarrassed to be watched.

One student will be the lecturer in this part, and his or her partner will act as interpreter. The first partner must use gibberish or nonsense words to explain one of the following tasks. The lecturer must take frequent pauses in the lecture in order to give the interpreter time to translate. The partners have no time to discuss or prepare what they will say, but they both know the topic. Encourage the lecturer to use lots of vocal inflection and facial expressions. The translator is, of course, just making up the interpretation, since the lecturer isn't really saying anything. If your lecturer is inhibited about making up nonsense words, then give them a random series of real words that they can just repeat over and over again.

Here are some lecture ideas to choose from:
- How to operate a small appliance
- How to tell friends that God loves them
- What to do when you're lost in the jungle
- What to do when you forget your homework
- What to do in a fire
- What you must do to be saved
- How to get to Alaska
- How to play lacrosse

Give other pairs a chance to lecture until everyone who would like to do so has had a turn. Hopefully the whole group will have some good laughs.

Curtain Call

We can't control how other people will react to the truths we share. We can only try to make God's message clear and understandable. Our own experience of God's love is something no one can deny. Lead a discussion using the following questions to help students reflect on the Bible lesson.

- **Did your shared lecture make any sense?** *(Answers will vary.)*
- **Those of you who gave lectures in gibberish, in what language were you actually thinking about what you would be saying?** *(English, most likely)*
- **Tell about a time when you were misunderstood.** *(Answers will vary.)*
- **Tell about a time when you shared your faith. Was it difficult to find the right words or make the person understand your meaning? Explain.** *(Answers will vary.)*
- **What do you think is the most important thing to tell other people about Jesus?** *(that He is the Son of God, that He is the only way to heaven, that He will forgive our sin if we ask Him)*

So is my word that goes out from my mouth: It will not return to me empty, but will accomplish what I desire and achieve the purpose for which I sent it.
Isaiah 55:11

Get'cha Power Here!

Scripture Verse:
Acts 19; 1 John 4:1-3a

Memory Verse:
You, dear children, are from God and have overcome them, because the one who is in you is greater than the one who is in the world.
1 John 4:4

Bible Background

God is not the only spiritual being with power. The spirits of darkness also have power, but God has infinitely more. Satan and his demons are subject to God's power. People who don't know God's power can easily be attracted by the powers of darkness. The Bible is full of images of demons as angels who joined the kingdom of Satan and rebelled against God. In particular, demons are a reality in the New Testament, where they are actively engaged in harassing God's people and trying to thwart His plans.

The people in Ephesus worshiped the goddess Artemis, but when Paul demonstrated that God's power was greater than that of Artemis, people turned to the true God. This affected the economy in Ephesus because people stopped buying shrines, idols, and religious souvenirs from the silversmiths.

The silversmiths got together and began to speak out publicly against Paul. They claimed to be defending Artemis, but more likely they were concerned with their pocketbooks. The silversmiths, more than anyone, knew the idols they made from silver had no real power of their own. They were more concerned about making money than knowing the truth. The sons of a man named Sceva even tried to cast out a demon by using the name of Jesus as a kind of magic spell or potion. They ended up being attacked by the man with the demon. God's power is not to be abused or treated lightly.

Isn't it astonishing to know that God's power is available to us? He lives in our hearts in the person of the Holy Spirit, whose power we can tap into for godly living and a victorious Christian life. We should be continually feeding the Spirit with regular prayer and times in His Word so that the power is always strong in us.

Teacher Tips

Students will work together in pairs or small groups to create a commercial. If you have a video camera available, plan to film the commercials. Filming typically motivates the kids to stay on task and do their best work. You will also end up with a recording you can view right away or plan to view at a later time when you can give it special focus—or even show it to parents.

Whenever choosing pairs or small groups, try to mix kids with various personalities and skills. Otherwise you may end up with all the shy kids in one group or all the leaders in another. Spread out the students who tend to be the creative ones into different groups.

Props

★ Video camera, if available

★ Costume box of jackets, vests, scarves, and hats for students to choose from

★ A bag of random items such as a hairbrush, garlic press, bottle of aftershave, feather duster, and so on

Set

Each pair or group needs a place where they can work away from others. Try to spread out into different areas as much as space will allow. To film or view the commercials, create a performance area with room for the class to watch each presentation.

Activity Instructions

Start by discussing commercials. Let students take turns telling about commercials they like or remember. Talk about the commercials and all the techniques that advertisers use to sell their product. Some examples are:

"Today" or "This week only"—you don't want to miss an opportunity
You'll be one of the fun or cool people
Catchy jingles that stick in your head
"4 out of 5 dentists recommend . . ."—expert opinions
Celebrity endorsements
Humor
Two for the price of one
Earn a free gift with a purchase of $30

Have students brainstorm more ideas. Discuss how advertisers' techniques often give misleading ideas or false impressions of what their product really offers. Optional: Have some sales circulars for kids to look at. What commercials portray or promise usually falls drastically short of reality.

Once students are in pairs or small groups, have each pair or group choose an object out of the bag. Remind them to take the first object their hands touch and not to go feeling around in the bag. If they like, they can shake the bag first.

Each pair or group will work together to create a commercial for the object they draw from the bag. The commercial will make it seem like the object is the most important and powerful possession anyone could have.

Encourage students to make all kinds of false promises about what this object can actually do, like a garlic press that will cook the whole meal for you and clean the kitchen afterward. Objects might even have unusual or magical power of some kind. Remind students to choose techniques from the brainstormed list to use in selling their products. All the products should be portrayed as having the power to "change your life." The students get to decide how.

Give the groups about ten minutes to work before performing the commercials for one another. Remind them not to spend much time in discussion or debate, but to jump right in and start trying their ideas. Provide pencil and paper in case they want to jot down any ideas or dialogue.

When the commercials are ready to be performed, set up a viewing and filming area. Remind the viewers to be a good audience by sitting quietly, withholding any comments, and concentrating on watching rather than on their own upcoming performances. This is especially important if you are filming, so you won't end up with background noise, although laughter is okay.

Curtain Call

Lead a discussion using the following questions to review the activity and tie in Bible truths about God's power.

- **If you could have one super power, what would you choose? Why?** *(Answers will vary.)*
- **Some people still believe that certain objects, like crystals or other symbols or objects, have power. What do you think?** *(Answers will vary.)*
- **In the book of Acts, people were healed just by touching the apostles' handkerchiefs. Was that magic?** *(No. It was through God's healing power.)*
- **Do you think it's possible for an object to contain evil power? Why or why not?** *(No. Objects don't have any power, although demons can use them to deceive us into believing they do.)*
- **In what ways have you experienced or witnessed God's power?** *(Answers will vary.)*

Remind your students that any power not from God is false power.

You, dear children, are from God and have overcome them, because the one who is in you is greater than the one who is in the world.
1 John 4:4

Steering the Conversation

Scripture Verse:
Acts 24:1—25:12

Memory Verse:
Always be prepared to give an answer to everyone who asks
you to give the reason for the hope that you have.
1 Peter 3:15b

Bible Background

Paul spent two years in prison because the Jews made up false charges against him. Over and over he was called before the governor, Felix, to explain and defend himself. Paul used these opportunities not only to disprove the charges against him, but to speak to Felix about truth, righteousness, and judgment. Felix didn't like this because he was a corrupt man, yet he continued to call for Paul. He was hoping Paul would offer him a bribe (Acts 24:26). Eventually Felix returned to Rome and was replaced by Festus.

The Jews thought that this was their chance to finally have Paul killed under a new governor. Paul was unafraid to share his message with Festus, and then he appealed to Caesar, giving him an opportunity to appear before the most powerful man in the Roman Empire.

Although Paul was falsely accused and underwent the hardship of prison, he didn't waste time feeling sorry for himself or angry about the injustice of his situation. He was thankful that God had given him the chance to speak the truth of Jesus before powerful people. He considered every situation an opportunity. God's Word encourages us to always be prepared to share the hope that we have.

Have you had recent opportunities to tell others the good news about Jesus? When we are prepared to share with others and we pray for "divine encounters," God will bring people to us who are desperate to know the truth about salvation. What a joy it is to be used by the King!

Teacher Tips

This is an improvisational exercise that requires some imagination. It's a good idea to demonstrate this activity for the group before you start. If you have a student with some creativity or dramatic flair, explain the exercise to that student ahead of time so that the two of you can model it. This will eliminate a lot of questions and confusion.

Props

★ Slips of paper with phrases from page 101
★ Chairs

Set

Set up a performance area with two or three chairs next to each other to represent a park bench. Unless you have a raised platform on which to put the park bench, audience members will see better sitting on the floor.

Activity Instructions

Paul was always ready to steer every conversation toward his favorite topic—the Gospel. And yet he did this by the power of the Holy Spirit. If we listen to the guiding of the Spirit, we can share in a more natural way.

In this activity students must steer the conversation in such a way that they can say assigned phrases in a natural way that makes sense. Two people sit on the bench. Person 1 opens the conversation using the phrase on his or her slip of paper. Person 2 must then respond to what Person 1 has said in a logical manner. The improvised conversation continues on with each person responding to whatever the other says. However, Person 2 must steer the conversation so that he or she can say the assigned phrase in the midst of the conversation. Once Person 2 has been able to say the assigned phrase, the scene ends.

Then Person 1 leaves the bench and Person 2 welcomes the next volunteer to sit on the bench. Person 2 will now start a new scene using the same phrase with which the last scene ended. This new scene will go a completely different direction as the new volunteer tries to steer it in a way that will fit his or her assigned line.

Here's an example of what an improvised scene might sound like. Some conversations will be longer than this and others will be shorter. You, as the leader, need to know the line each new volunteer has on his or her paper so that you can call "Cut!" when you hear it said. Also, you can coach students if they're having trouble. *Assigned lines are in bold in this sample.* Use this sample as a demonstration.

Person 1: I never eat them without mustard.
Person 2: I feel the same way. They're just kind of bland otherwise.
Person 1: A lot of people find it strange, you know. Most people have never tried mustard on a banana.
Person 2: *(hears banana and has an idea of how to steer toward her line)* I know. I actually only tried it by accident.
Person 1: What happened?
Person 2: Well, I peeled a banana to put in my cereal and when I walked over to get a knife I didn't realize that the banana peel had fallen off the counter and I slipped on it and ended up sticking the banana right in the open mustard jar where my brother was packing his lunch. It looked kind of good, so I tried it. **That was my great discovery.**

Curtain Call

Lead a discussion using the following questions to review the activity and tie in Bible truths about how we can share our faith naturally.

- **Have you ever tried to share your faith? Why or why not? What were the results?** *(Answers will vary.)*
- **How did you feel when you were sharing?** *(nervous, excited, afraid of rejection)*
- **What other exciting news have you shared with your friends?** *(Answers will vary.)*
- **Was that easier or more difficult than sharing about Jesus? Why or why not?** *(Answers will vary.)*
- **How can you be prepared to share?** *(know why you believe what you believe, study God's Word, memorize Scripture)*

Copy this page and cut phrases into slips of paper.

It was then that the trouble really began.

I've got a pet frog named Homer.

All I need is twenty-five dollars.

If it ain't broke, don't fix it.

I thought I was going to die.

They just don't write them like that anymore.

My neighbor chews tobacco, too.

Why don't you just try it once?

Hasn't anyone ever told you that before?

What can it hurt?

And all I said was, "Please pass the butter."

And you know, I couldn't tell the difference.

Walk a mile in my shoes.

I've never been so embarrassed!

You're kidding—she's my sister!

And ever since I've had this nervous twitch.

Always be prepared
to give an answer to everyone who
asks you to give the reason
for the hope that
you have.
1 Peter 3:15b

Oh, That's Good;
Oh, That's Bad

Scripture Verse:

Acts 27:1—28:16

Memory Verse:

Cast your cares on the LORD and he will sustain you;
he will never let the righteous fall.
Psalm 55:22

Bible Background

Paul was probably happy to finally be leaving the prison in Caesarea and to be joined again by his traveling companion, Luke. They were sent by ship, under guard, to state Paul's case before Caesar in Rome, the capital of the empire. They stopped in Sidon, and Paul was even allowed to visit his friends. Things were finally going well for Paul.

But then the centurion in charge ignored Paul's warning that they shouldn't sail at that time of year, and they ended up in a terrible storm at sea. Everyone aboard thought they were done for, but God promised Paul they would all be spared. Trying to escape a vicious storm that lasted for weeks, the ship's crew finally made a run for shore. Unfortunately, the ship hit a sandbar and was beaten to pieces by the pounding surf. But God's promise held true, and all 276 passengers made it safely to shore.

Then, while gathering firewood, Paul was bitten by a poisonous snake. The people of the island thought he must be a murderer and the snakebite was God's justice. However, Paul shook the snake off and didn't even get sick. The islanders decided Paul must be a god and started to worship him. Talk about some ups and downs!

Our lives are filled with ups and downs, even though they may not be as dramatic as the ones described in Acts. But we can learn from Paul's reaction to his circumstances. He was calm and fearless because he had complete faith in God. Even though we don't have angels speaking to us as Paul did, we do have the Word of God which speaks to us each time we read and study it. Fill your mind and heart with His Word, and when the "hard times" come, you will be as calm and fearless as the Apostle Paul!

Teacher Tips

The "fortunately, unfortunately" or "that's good, that's bad" motif is common in children's stories. If time permits it would be fun to read one—or part of one—such story, as an introduction to this activity. You can find several such stories by searching your local library or online.

You can use a bell or sound signal in place of passing the ball. This gives you as the teacher control over when a student stops talking. That way you can stop a student right in the middle of a sentence and see how the next person chooses to finish the thought.

Props

★ Any kind of ball that can be rolled across the circle to indicate the next person to speak
★ Pencils
★ Small slips of paper
★ Two bowls or containers

Set

This activity works best if students are seated in a circle on the floor. Clear the chairs away to make space for a large circle.

Activity Instructions

Distribute a pencil and two slips of paper to each student. Have students write on one slip of paper the name and description of a person. This is not a real person, just a made-up character. Ask them to include at least one describing feature. For example: Betsy, a seven-year-old girl with bright red hair.

Next, ask the students to write on the second slip of paper some kind of task, chore, or quest that must be completed. Remind them not to include anything gross, embarrassing, or violent. For example: must find a way across the river where there is food, or must find lost dog.

Collect the slips of paper in two separate bowls or containers and instruct students to sit in a circle on the floor. Once everyone is settled, draw one slip of paper from each container. One slip will tell you the main character of your story and the other will tell you what task your character must complete. You hold the ball and begin the story. Explain the process as follows, substituting the character and situation you've drawn from the bowls for Betsy and the lost dog.

Okay, our story is about Betsy, a seven-year-old girl with bright red hair. Betsy must find her lost dog. While searching for her dog, many different things will happen to Betsy. Some will be good and some will be bad. When I roll the ball to you it will be your turn to add three or more sentences to the story. Remember that whatever you add can't be gross, embarrassing, or violent. You can't kill Betsy or her dog. You also can't change anything that has already happened, so if Betsy catches her hair in a tree branch and has to cut it off, it can't magically grow back with the next storyteller.

We will take turns having good and bad things happen to Betsy, just like what happened to the Apostle Paul on his journey to appear before Caesar. Every other person will start by saying, "Fortunately" or "Unfortunately" to start the next portion of the story. If the person before you starts with "Fortunately" and adds something good for Betsy, then whoever that person rolls the ball to must start with "Unfortunately" and add something bad for Betsy. When we've all had at least one turn to add something, we will end the story with Betsy accomplishing her task because God is on her side.

Roll the ball in random order so that no one is sure who will be picked to tell the next portion of the story. However, as the teacher, keep track and make sure everyone gets a turn. After the group has told a story, you can start a new one by drawing two more slips out of the containers. Try one of the following variations each time you tell a new story, in order to make the activity more challenging and interesting.

Variation 1—Draw two character slips and one task to give your character a partner.

Variation 2—Every third or fourth person should draw a new character out of the first container and add that person into the story. The new characters can either help or hinder the main character.

Variation 3—Start out with two characters and two tasks. Somehow the two characters meet and either help each other or create an obstacle for the other to complete his or her task.

Curtain Call

Use the following questions to lead a discussion about how we respond to the ups and downs of life.

In all the ups and downs that Paul experienced on his journey to Rome he never got discouraged or questioned God. He knew that whatever happened was part of God's plan to give him opportunities to further God's kingdom. He was more concerned about God's message than his own welfare.

- Have you ever had something bad happen that turned out for the best? How? *(Answers will vary.)*
- Think of an unfortunate event that taught you an important lesson. Can you share it? *(Answers will vary.)*
- Why does God allow misfortune, pain, and inconvenience in our lives? *(to help us rely on Him, to further His kingdom, to grow our faith)*
- The Bible tells us that God tests and tries our faith to make it stronger. How is faith like a muscle that must be exercised? *(It must be used, or it will grow weak. It has to be fed good food to become strong.)*
- How can our faith in God during trials encourage others? *(They see God at work in our lives. They recognize that such faith is supernatural.)*

Cast your cares on the LORD
and he will sustain you;
he will never let the
righteous fall.
Psalm 55:22

Together to the Finish

Scripture Verse:
Philippians 1:19–27; 2 Timothy 4:6–8; Romans 12:1–2

Memory Verse:
I press on toward the goal to win the prize for which
God has called me heavenward in Christ Jesus.
Philippians 3:14

Bible Background

Paul was imprisoned in Rome while he awaited trial. In this case, he was probably under house arrest and lived with some degree of comfort. Friends were able to attend to his needs. Paul wrote to the Philippians from Rome. That letter reflects Paul's passion for God when he says, "To live is Christ and to die is gain" (Philippians 1:21).

Paul was ready to meet his Lord through death, not because he'd lived a perfect life, but because he trusted in God's grace to cover his sin. He held onto that belief adamantly to the end of his days. For Paul, his faith was not a passing phase or something that just made life "work" for him. Christ was his very reason for living.

Paul's second letter to Timothy emerged out of a different kind of imprisonment. Paul most likely wrote this letter from the Mamertine jail where he was being held prisoner under deprived conditions. He was chained up in a cold dungeon like a murderer or thief.

Perhaps Paul knew that his life on earth was drawing to a close when he wrote, "I have fought the good fight, I have finished the race, I have kept the faith" (2 Timothy 4:7). According to church tradition, Paul was executed shortly after he wrote this letter. But even in his awareness that he might not survive this imprisonment, Paul held onto his faith.

Do you have that kind of faith—the kind that endures even to the brink of death? Thank God today for the gift of faith He has given you and ask Him to strengthen it more and more each day. Then when you are tested as Paul was, you can "keep the faith," as he did.

Teacher Tips

This is a wonderful role-playing and team-building exercise. In addition to reinforcing the Bible lesson and affording dramatic expression, it is effective for unifying a group and teaching about accepting differences in other people.

The students will be working in groups of no less than five. You could have up to eight per group depending on your numbers. Emphasize to the students that they are responsible for their teammates and the number one goal is to keep each other safe.

Props

★ Variety of bandanas and larger scarves to be used as blindfolds and slings

★ Masking tape

★ Slips of paper with disabilities—Make several copies of page 109, cut the descriptions apart, and place them in a bowl.

Set

You need a really large space for this activity. If possible, it is best to do it outside in an open, grassy area. Asphalt or concrete will increase the possibility of injury.

Decide on a race route in the available area. If there are obstacles to go around, over, or under, so much the better; it will increase the challenge. If you do this in a large indoor area or gymnasium, you can set up obstacles using tables, chairs, or other barriers.

Using the masking tape, mark off a starting line and a finish line. The same line can indicate both start and finish if you are having teams go around a building or loop back in the same direction.

Activity Instructions

Once students are divided into small groups of five or more, have them sit down with their group for the explanation of the activity before going outside.

In a moment we will go outside and your team will be racing the other team(s) to get to the finish line. However, every person on the team will have some kind of weakness or disability. Your goal as a team is to somehow work together to make up for each other's weaknesses and to get your whole team across the finish line. No one can win on his or her own.

In order for a team to win, they must all cross the finish line together with everyone touching. Everyone in the group must be physically attached to the rest of the group. A team can only win if no members are hurt or left behind. And no one can cheat with a disability. For example, if you are supposed to be blind, no peeking.

At this point you can have each person draw a slip of paper from the bowl, assigning a disability. As soon as students open their slips of paper and read what's on them, they should begin to role-play. Those who are blind should have a team member blindfold them. Those who are deaf should stop responding to anything spoken. Those who are missing limbs should tie up a limb in a scarf as a sling.

Your first job is to get your whole team safely to the starting line. There are members of your team who can't hear what I am saying right now and don't understand what's happening. There are members who can't see where they are going and others who can't walk to get there. Decide right now how you will help each other and follow me out to the starting line.

When all the teams are assembled at the starting line, you can demonstrate or explain the course. If they must go around, under, or over certain obstacles, either you or a student can demonstrate. Explain to the teams once again that they are not to cheat on their disabilities. They can proceed through the course however it works best for them, but they must cross the finish line in one big group with everyone physically attached to some part of the group. Emphasize again that all members must be kept safe and unharmed. Ask if there are questions, and when you feel confident that everyone understands, start the race.

When the race is finished, go back inside or sit down in a comfortable area for a discussion time.

Copy this page and cut descriptions into slips of paper

You are blind.

You are deaf.

You have no arms.

You can't speak.

You have only one leg.

Mentally handicapped—you can't understand.

You can't walk.

You are blind and deaf.

Curtain Call

We all have weaknesses. Some are physical and others are psychological, mental, emotional, or spiritual. When Paul talked about finishing the race, he wasn't satisfied to cross the finish line alone. He wanted to take as many other people with him as he could by helping believers keep their faith strong to the end of their lives. He established churches so that people could help one another in communities. We are not meant to walk our journey of faith all alone.

Discuss the following questions to help students process their experience and connect to biblical truths.

- **Did anyone in your team get hurt or left behind? Why or why not?** *(Answers will vary.)*
- **Were any of you frightened at any time during the race? Tell us about it.** *(Answers will vary.)*
- **What kinds of things did you say to encourage each other to keep going despite your weaknesses?** *(Answers will vary.)*
- **How did it feel when your team crossed the finish line together?** *(awesome, rewarding, etc.)*

Remind students that Christ rewards everyone who loves Him to the end.

I press on toward the goal to win the prize for which God has called me heavenward in Christ Jesus. Philippians 3:14

Topic Index

Scripture Index

Classy, Flashy Bible Dramas for Tweens